I've Got Questions

Ashley Irby

Dedication

This book is dedicated to my professor, Dr. Eddie Burris. You taught me that all the answers I'll ever need for my life are in the book of Proverbs.

Also available from Springs of Life Publishing Company:

Love, the Greatest Force Ever &
Conquering Insecurities, Angie Cleveland
Excuse Me, Your Rejection is Showing, Kevin Shelton
My Perfect Peace, Kelly Williams
Pieces of Me, Ashley May

I've Got Questions

Ashley Irby

Springs of Life Publishing Company books are available for special quantity discounts to use as premiums and sale promotions, or for use in corporate/ church training programs. For more information please write to the Special Sales Director:

SOLP Bulk Training Sales

PO Box 170726

Spartanburg SC 29301

Table of Contents

How can I become a multimillionaire? What's the most powerful weapon on the face of the earth? Is it possible to murder someone without physically killing them? Does the Bible say anything about text messaging? As I studied the book of Proverbs I found the answer to questions like these and many more. If you have questions the book of Proverbs has the answers. I pray that you enjoy this book as much as I did writing it!

~ Ashley Irby

Proverbs 1

Reader: Why was the book of Proverbs written?
Answer: So that men and women can live successful lives. [Proverbs1:1-6]

Reader: What does it mean to fear God?
Answer: Fearing God means you have respect for the Lord. You live your life in a way that honors and pleases Him. [Proverbs 1:7]

Reader: Should I listen to my parents when they give me advice?
Answer: Yes. What you learn from them will keep you from making the same mistakes they made when they were your age. [Proverbs 1:8-9]

Reader: What should I do if a person tries to get me to sin?
Answer: Don't listen to them. A lot of times people will do things just to be part of the crowd and look cool. Peer pressure has caused lots of people to do things they later regretted. [Proverbs 1:10-18]

Reader: What can cause a person to put their life in danger?

Answer: Being greedy for money. [Proverbs 1:19]

Reader: Who is the lady in the first chapter of Proverbs?

Answer: Her name is Wisdom. It's very important that you listen to her and do what she says. She wants to make you wise and teach you right from wrong. She doesn't want to see you make a mess of your life. She wants you to be successful. If you ignore her when you need her she won't be there for you, but if you listen to her and take her advice she will bless you and protect you from evil. [Proverbs 1:20-33]

Proverbs 2

Reader: How should I feel about learning God's commands?
Answer: You should treasure them. Concentrate on learning them and putting them into practice. Once you do you'll develop the fear of God. [Proverbs 2:1-6]

Reader: If I want God to bless me and make me successful what do I need to do?
Answer: Practice integrity. Integrity is doing the right thing when no one is looking and not having secret sins in your life. [Proverbs 2:7-8]

Reader: What's a benefit of having integrity?
Answer: Integrity will keep you from making bad decisions that could ruin your life. [Proverbs 2:9-11]

Reader: What will wisdom do for my life?
Answer: She will protect you from people that want to see you fall and be unsuccessful. They talk like they have your best interest at heart, but they really don't. [Proverbs 2:12]

Reader: How can I spot such people?
Answer: Their words are crooked. They say one thing, but they do another. They also enjoy sinning. If someone tries to get you to sin they're not your friend. [Proverbs 2:13-15]

Reader: How can I avoid committing adultery?
Answer: If a married woman compliments you don't dwell on what she says. Also, if a married woman invites you to her house and her husband is not home don't go. You don't know what her motives are. [Proverbs 2:16-19]

Reader: Who should I get advice from about marriage?
Answer: Couples that have a thriving marriage. They'll help you become a great future spouse and prepare you for marriage. [Proverbs 2:20-22]

Proverbs 3

Reader: If I want to live a long time and have a satisfying life, what should I do?
Answer: Continue to study the Bible and obey God. [Proverbs 3:1]

Reader: How can obeying God cause me to live longer?
Answer: Sin cuts your life short. Obedience prolongs it. [Proverbs 3:2]

Reader: What can I do to experience favor on my job?
Answer: Be loyal and kind to your coworkers and your boss. [Proverbs 3:3-4]

Reader: There are several situations that I have going on in my life right now that I don't know what to do about.
Answer: Trust God with the situation and pray about it. He will show you what His will is and which path to take. [Proverbs 3:5-6]

Reader: What happens when someone decides to stop an addiction?

Answer: Your mind and body will become cleansed, strong, and healthy. [Proverbs 3:7-8]

Reader: How does God feel about tithing?
Answer: Tithing triggers faith, and God loves faith! [Proverbs 3:9-10]

Reader: When God corrects me after I've done something wrong how should I take it?
Answer: Be happy about it. It shows that God loves you and cares about you. He's treating you like His own child. [Proverbs 3:11-12]

Reader: Is it possible to experience heaven on earth?
Answer: Yes, but only if you seek wisdom. [Proverbs 3:13]

Reader: What should I desire more than money?
Answer: Wisdom. If you seek her more than seeking money she will honor you, make you rich, and lengthen your life. [Proverbs 3:14-18]

Reader: Did wisdom play a role in creation?
Answer: Yes. God used wisdom to create the entire world. [Proverbs 3:19-20]

Reader: How can I maintain the wisdom that I get from God?
Answer: You must guard it with your life. You do this by meditating and practicing the Word of God daily. [Proverbs 3:21]

Reader: What will happen if I do this?
Answer: You won't have to be afraid of evil people because God will protect you from them. Another reward is that you'll sleep better at night because you'll have fewer worries. [Proverbs 3:22-26]

Reader: Is it smart to help people in need?
Answer: Only if you can. Don't lie to them and say you're going to help them when you can't. [Proverbs 3:27-28]

Reader: Is it a good idea to pick a fight with someone who hasn't done anything to me?
Answer: No. You never want to intentionally make enemies. [Proverbs 3:29-30]

Reader: What can I do to be God's friend?
Answer: Don't copy the behavior of people who are evil and violent. [Proverbs 3:31-32]

Reader: Will God give me a housewarming gift for being godly?

Answer: Yes. Your housewarming gift will be favor and protection. [Proverbs 3:33]

Reader: If I want God's favor on my life what do I need to do?

Answer: Be humble. Never think that you know more than God. [Proverbs 3:34]

Reader: If I behave foolishly what should I expect?

Answer: Shame and regret. [Proverbs 3:35]

Reader: If I behave wisely what will happen?

Answer: God will honor you. [Proverbs 3:35]

Proverbs 4

Reader: What should parents teach their children to do at an early age?
Answer: Take God's Word seriously. [Proverbs 4:1-4]

Reader: How should I view Lady Wisdom?
Answer: As your bride. If you love her she will protect you. [Proverbs 4:5-6]

Reader: What's the first step to seeking Lady Wisdom?
Answer: You must realize her value. If you prize her and put her above everything else in your life she will honor and bless you. [Proverbs 4:7-9]

Reader: How can I avoid premature death?
Answer: Take the advice that she gives you and don't reject it. [Proverbs 4:10]

Reader: Is there anything Lady Wisdom can't do?
Answer: She can't force you to follow the right path. You must choose. [Proverbs 4:11]

Reader: If I listen to her what'll happen?

Answer: You'll make better decisions with ease. [Proverbs 4:12]

Reader: How can I show Lady Wisdom that I love her?
Answer: Listen to what she tells you and don't take her for granted. [Proverbs 4:13]

Reader: What do criminals do all day long?
Answer: They think of ways to commit crimes. [Proverbs 4:14-17]

Reader: I'm upset because I'm single and not married yet. What should I do?
Answer: If you want to find a spouse you must let your light shine. You do this by becoming the person you're looking for. [Proverbs 4:18-19]

Reader: What should I do after reading the bible?
Answer: Think about what you've read. Your mind will be sharp which will cause your body to function better. [Proverbs 4:20-22]

Reader: Why should I guard my mind?
Answer: When you think about things you shouldn't you abuse yourself emotionally. When

you think positive thoughts, you strengthen yourself emotionally which will make you a happier person. [Proverbs 4:23]

Reader: Is there anything wrong with listening to people grumble and complain all the time?
Answer: Stay away from people who complain a lot. If you don't you will end up like them.
[Proverbs 4:24]

Reader: What can I do to make sure I accomplish my goals?
Answer: Write your goals down and look at them daily. Don't compare yourself to others that are further along than you are. If there is something in your life that you know might distract you from accomplishing your goals stay away from it.
[Proverbs 4:25-27]

Proverbs 5

Reader: How can I protect myself from committing adultery?
Answer: Listen to the advice the Bible gives you. [Proverbs 5:1-2]

Reader: What is a sign that a person is willing to sleep with me even though they know I'm married?
Answer: They will flirt with you and give you compliments. They will say things like, "I wish my spouse was more like you. Your spouse is lucky to be married to you." [Proverbs 5:3]

Reader: What is committing adultery like?
Answer: It's the same thing as drinking poison or stabbing yourself with a knife. [Proverbs 5:4]

Reader: What does an unfaithful spouse and hell have in common?
Answer: The person who commits adultery will suffer just like an individual who is in hell. [Proverbs 5:5]

Reader: What can I do to prevent myself from cheating on my spouse?

Answer: Think about the consequences. [Proverbs 5:6]

Reader: If my spouse is out of town do I need to invite friends over to keep me company?
Answer: If the person is the same sex as you then it's okay. If the person is not the same sex as you don't do it. [Proverbs 5:7-8]

Reader: What are the consequences for a spouse that cheats?
Answer: Five things will happen:
1. Your spouse and children will lose respect for you.
2. You'll be remembered as a hypocrite and a liar.
3. You'll lose money in court when your spouse divorces you.
4. You'll experience severe depression.
5. Your reputation will be damaged. [Proverbs 5:9-14]

Reader: What does water have to do with marriage?
Answer: Your body needs water to survive. If you're dehydrated your body will break down. The

same thing is true in marriage. You should hydrate one another sexually so that your marriage will be healthy. [Proverbs 5:15]

Reader: Right now, I'm single. What can I do to prepare sexually for my spouse?
Answer: Reserve all your sexual energy and passion for your future spouse. [Proverbs 5:16-17]

Reader: What does my wife want me to do on a consistent basis?
Answer: Compliment her on her appearance. [Proverbs 5:18]

Reader: What can I do to show my husband I love him?
Answer: Allow him to enjoy your body. [Proverbs 5:19]

Reader: What is mental adultery?
Answer: It's when you fantasize about having sex with someone other than your spouse. [Proverbs 5:20]

Reader: Who do I need to be worried about the most when it comes to adultery?

Answer: God. Even though others might not be able to see what you're doing He does. [Proverbs 5:21]

Reader: Is there anything single men and women can do to stay away from sexual sin?
Answer: Develop discipline. Don't let your sex drive control you. You control it. [Proverbs 5:22-23]

Proverbs 6

Reader: Should I take on the debt of someone else by taking out a loan for them?
Answer: No. You will be placing yourself in financial bondage for years to come. If you can't afford to give them the money they need don't cosign for them to get a loan. Don't put you and your spouse's finances at risk just to please another person that's gotten themselves into financial trouble. [Proverbs 6:1-5]

Reader: Sometimes I get lazy and put stuff off. How can I become more disciplined?
Answer: Have you ever studied ants? Ants don't need anyone to supervise them to get their work done. They have inner motivation. You should learn how to work hard when no one is watching. When something needs to be done take the initiative and do the task right away. [Proverbs 6:6-8]

Reader: Is it important to rest when you're tired?
Answer: There should be a healthy balance. You don't want to lie in bed and sleep all day long. When you sleep too long it puts you behind on reaching your goals. [Proverbs 6:9-11]

Reader: How can I tell if someone is a con artist?
Answer: They try to gain your confidence with friendly smiles and flattery, but they're plotting evil against you. They're smooth talkers. They will go to any length to convince you to do something they know you don't want to do. These kinds of people want you to make quick decisions without thinking first. Never be in a hurry to do anything. Always think it through. [Proverbs 6:12-14]

Reader: Will God punish them for their actions?
Answer: Yes. It'll be unexpected; they won't see it coming. [Proverbs 6:15]

Reader: Is there anything that God can't stand?
Answer: There are seven things He hates:
1. People that are prideful and stuck on themselves.
2. People that twist the truth. Distorting the truth to get the upper hand is lying.
3. People that kill innocent people.
4. People who come up with evil schemes to hurt others.
5. People who get excited to commit sin.

6. People who lie on others, especially in legal matters.
7. People who cause division among their family members. [Proverbs 6:16-19]

Reader: How important is it that I rely on God's Word and do what He says?
Answer: It's very important. Always review and study the things that God teaches you. If you do you will sleep better at night because you'll have peace that you're living your life the way God wants you to. You'll know what to do when situations arise because you'll have God's Word in your heart to help you make right decisions. God will make your life easier because He will help you avoid sins that could jeopardize your life and cut it short, especially the sin of adultery. [Proverbs 6:20-24]

Reader: How can I avoid a person who is trying to seduce me to sleep with them?
Answer: Don't think about their flattering words and dwell on how good they look. [Proverbs 6:25]

Reader: What could happen if I sleep with a married person?

Answer: You could lose your life and die. [Proverbs 6:26]

Reader: I know some people who has cheated on their spouse and haven't been caught.
Answer: Just because they haven't been caught doesn't mean they won't. They're playing with fire, and eventually they will get caught. [Proverbs 6:27-29]

Reader: How does God feel about adultery?
Answer: God takes marriage seriously. When you cause another person to break their marriage covenant this angers God. You can't cheat with a married woman and expect not to go unpunished. The husband of the woman you cheated with won't be satisfied until he gets revenge. He might even try to murder you. [Proverbs 6:30-35]

Proverbs 7

Reader: How can wisdom protect me from having an affair?
Answer: When people flatter you and try to flirt with you, wisdom will give you the strength to resist them so you won't end up like the young man in Proverbs chapter seven. [Proverbs 7:1-5]

Reader: What happened to him?
Answer: He was walking the streets at night and a married woman approached him. She was dressed to kill. She flattered him and told him that she wanted him to sleep with her. When her husband came up in the conversation she convinced the young man that he wouldn't find out because he was out of town on a business trip. He went to her house and had sex with her. He ended up dying a short time later. [Proverbs 7:6-27]

Reader: How can I avoid falling into the same trap?
Answer: You should practice the "3T" system.

Reader: What's the "3T" system?
Answer: It's a way to resist sexual temptation. Joseph used it when he resisted sleeping with

Potiphar's wife. The first "T" is time. Joseph stayed away from her and didn't spend time alone with her. He stayed out of her way as much as possible. Don't spend time alone with the opposite sex. Activities like going to lunch or dinner together are off limits.

Reader: What's the second "T"?
Answer: Talk. Joseph didn't talk to Potiphar's wife. Conversation is how most affairs start. The more you talk to a woman that's not your wife, or a man that's not your husband, the more attracted you will become to them. Don't have phone conversations or exchange emails. If you both work at the same job, talk about work only.

Reader: What's the last "T"?
Answer: Touch. When Potiphar's wife tried to touch Joseph, he ran. Don't allow a man or woman to touch you sexually. Remember H and H, hugs and hands. Don't give hugs and hold hands with a person that's not your spouse.

Proverbs 8

Reader: Who's the greatest woman in the world?
Answer: Lady Wisdom. She knows everything. Everything she says is right. She's never been wrong about anything ever! If you focus on pursuing her she will make your life awesome. [Proverbs 8:1-9]

Reader: How do I pursue her?
Answer: Listen to what she says, memorize it, and put it into practice. She's the most precious asset you'll ever have. No amount of money can compare to what she's worth. For starters, she hates evil. She doesn't like people who are prideful and arrogant. It disgusts her. [Proverbs 8:10-13]

Reader: How can she help me?
Answer: She can give you the insights and intelligence that she gives to leaders across the globe. Whenever you see godly leaders flourishing it's because of her help. If you love her she will love you back. Pursuing her won't be a waste of time. It will be time well spent! She'll bless you in ways you never imagined. [Proverbs 8:14-21]

Reader: How was she created?
Answer: God formed her before He made the world. She was the first thing He made. She was right by God's side when He created the sky, mountains and oceans. Everything God created she enjoyed. [Proverbs 8:22-31]

Reader: How do I pursue her?
Answer: Spend time with her every day. She should be the first person you have contact with when you wake up. If you put her first in your life you will have God's favor on your life. [Proverbs 8:32-35]

Reader: What if I don't put her first in my life?
Answer: You curse yourself. [Proverbs 8:36]

Proverbs 9

Reader: What kind of house does Lady Wisdom have?
Answer: She has a mansion. It's beautiful. She loves to invite men and women to her house to eat with her. [Proverbs 9:1]

Reader: What kind of food does she serve?
Answer: She doesn't serve physical food; she serves spiritual food. When you listen to her advice and do what she says it nourishes the Holy Spirit living inside of you. [Proverbs 9:2-6]

Reader: How do wicked people respond to correction?
Answer: They hate it; they think they know it all. Don't try to correct these kinds of people. They'll get angry at you. [Proverbs 9:7-8]

Reader: How do wise people respond to correction?
Answer: They love it! They understand that they're not perfect and need advice from others. When you correct the wise they will thank you for it. [Proverbs 9:8-9]

Reader: Why is the fear of the Lord so important?
Answer: It will help you look at situations from God's point of view, which will result in you making wise decisions. [Proverbs 9:10]

Reader: Can wisdom prolong my life?
Answer: Yes, she can prevent you from putting yourself in dangerous situations. [Proverbs 10:11]

Reader: If I become wise who will benefit from it?
Answer: Primarily you. Your life will be blessed. [Proverbs 10:12]

Reader: What if I don't listen to her?
Answer: Your life will be cursed. [Proverbs 10:12]

Reader: There is a woman named Folly in chapter nine. Can you tell me about her?
Answer: She's ignorant and stupid. She's the opposite of Lady Wisdom. She doesn't care about your life. She wants you to do things in secret that'll put your life in serious danger. [Proverbs 9:13-18]

Proverbs 10

Reader: Will the choices I make affect my parents?
Answer: Yes. If you live a godly life your mother
and father will be proud of you. [Proverbs 10:1]

Reader: If a person earns their money by cheating
people and being dishonest what'll happen to the
money they earn?
Answer: They could end up being killed by the
person they cheated. They'll want revenge for
being robbed of their money. People who are
honest and practice integrity in business don't have
to worry about this. [Proverbs 10:2]

Reader: If people are hungry to be successful in life
will God bless them with success?
Answer: If you're godly, yes. If you're evil, no.
[Proverbs 10:3]

Reader: I know plenty of ungodly people that are
rich and successful.
Answer: It won't last. Financial success is one thing,
but spiritual success is even better. When godly
people achieve success God gives them the peace
and health to enjoy it. When evil people achieve

success they often don't have any peace. [Proverbs 10:3]

Reader: Why is that?
Answer: They are afraid that it'll all be taken from them at any moment. [Proverbs 10:3]

Reader: I want to be a multi-millionaire one day. How can I accomplish this goal?
Answer: Solve a problem no one has solved. [Proverbs 10:4]

Reader: If I want to be successful how should I spend my summers?
Answer: A lot of people relax in the summer time. They become lazy and don't take advantage of their time. During summer, the days are longer. You have more daylight to get things done. Use your summers to accomplish your goals. [Proverbs 10:5]

Reader: What is something that godly people receive from God?
Answer: Blessings. [Proverbs 10:6]

Reader: What do evil people get?

Answer: They don't receive anything from God because they speak evil against Him. [Proverbs 10:6]

Reader: When someone godly dies how are they remembered?
Answer: They will be remembered for the love they showed to their family and friends. [Proverbs 10:7]

Reader: How are wicked people remembered?
Answer: They won't be remembered. After they die people forget all about them. [Proverbs 10:7]

Reader: If I want to be wise, what should I do?
Answer: Be open to learning from others. People who don't like listening to others fall flat on their faces because they think they know it all. [Proverbs 10:8]

Reader: How can I safe guard myself from being a hypocrite?
Answer: Have integrity. Hypocrites like to hide their sins so no one will find out, but eventually they'll get exposed. [Proverbs 10:9]

Reader: How should I respond to salesmen?

Answer: Be cautious. If they try to force you to buy their product say no. If they try to offer you a dishonest deal and they're winking and smiling about it say no. They're trying to deceive you. [Proverbs 10:10]

Reader: What kind of words do I need to speak to others?
Answer: Think of your mouth as a beautiful fountain with clean spring water flowing into a pond. Everyone loves pure water because it's refreshing. That's how your words should be. They should refresh people and lift people up. Evil people's mouths are muddy. Their words are dirty and disgusting. [Proverbs 10:11]

Reader: Why do some married couples argue all the time?
Answer: They don't know how to love each other unconditionally. [Proverbs 10:12]

Reader: How can I tell if a person is wise or foolish?
Answer: Listen to their speech. [Proverbs 10:13]

Reader: How do wise people grow in wisdom?

Answer: They spend time reading the Bible and books about God. Foolish people hate reading the Bible and learning about God. They consider it a waste of time. [Proverbs 10:14]

Reader: Is being financially secure important?
Answer: There is nothing wrong with having financial security. The problem occurs when people start trusting in their money more than they trust in God. They start to believe their money can take care of all their problems. [Proverbs 10:15]

Reader: What about poor people?
Answer: Some people are poor because of their own bad decisions. They've made bad investments or they are too lazy to work. Other people are poor because of unexpected events like the loss of a job or a health issue that won't allow them to work. These are the kinds of people God wants you to help. If you can help them out by buying them groceries or helping them with their bills do it. They need all the help they can get. [Proverbs 10:15]

Reader: How do godly people spend their money?

Answer: They give to God by tithing, pay their bills and expenses, put money in the bank for savings, and enjoy the rest. [Proverbs 10:16]

Reader: How do foolish people spend their money?
Answer: They squander it on getting credit cards they can't afford, eating out all the time, and buying unnecessary things they don't need. They have no clue how to budget. [Proverbs 10:16]

Reader: It's hard listening to someone that corrects you.
Answer: It is, but if you listen to their correction it could save you from heart ache and pain in the future. People who are too prideful to admit they're wrong destroy relationships. If you've done something wrong admit it and apologize. [Proverbs 10:17]

Reader: Why do foolish people pretend to like you when they really don't?
Answer: They flatter people they don't like to gain their confidence so they can hurt you later. If you see people who smile in people's faces and talk behind their back stay away from them. They will do the same to you. [Proverbs 10:18]

Reader: Can talking too much be a bad thing?
Answer: Yes, because it will lead to you gossiping about someone. It's better for you to be quiet and reserved when it comes to talking about others. If you don't have anything good to say just be quiet. [Proverbs 10:19]

Reader: How valuable are my words?
Answer: Good speech is like silver because you give valuable knowledge to people. But the words of foolish people are worthless. They don't have a wise thing to say about anything. [Proverbs 10:20]

Reader: If someone is down, how can I pick them up?
Answer: Encourage them with your words. Foolish people make the situation worse by scolding the person and putting them down even more. [Proverbs 10:21]

Reader: Can being rich be a bad thing?
Answer: Not for the godly. When God blesses godly people with wealth they can enjoy it because they realize the source of their wealth is God and not themselves. [Proverbs 10:22]

Reader: Why do some people enjoy sin?
Answer: They find it fun. They don't realize the danger of what they are doing. People who are wise sin too, but they hate it when they do. They repent of their sins and try to learn from their mistakes. [Proverbs 10:23]

Reader: Why is it that people who sin are paranoid all the time.
Answer: They're afraid of being found out and exposed. The godly are the exact opposite. They have continual peace because they have nothing to hide. That's why God blesses people who have integrity. [Proverbs 10:24]

Reader: What happens to wicked people when storms come into their life?
Answer: The storms destroy them. When storms come into godly people's lives they're able to stand and not be destroyed because God protects them. [Proverbs 10:25]

Reader: Should I get a lazy person to do something important for me?

Answer: No, because it will never get done and you will end up having to do it yourself. [Proverbs 10:26]

Reader: What's one of the greatest blessings the Lord can give me?
Answer: A long life. Engaging in sinful activities will cut your life short. [Proverbs 10:27]

Reader: How does God feel about my hopes and dreams for the future?
Answer: He wants to make them a reality, but if you sin against God and disobey Him the future that you want will never come to pass. [Proverbs 10:28]

Reader: Can God protect me from danger?
Answer: Yes, He can, but you must stay in His will. If you go outside the will of God you leave God's protection. [Proverbs 10:29]

Reader: Why does God talk about trees so much in the Bible?
Answer: Trees symbolize success. When you see a tree flourishing and growing it's because its roots are strong. When your roots are strong in God your

life will flourish! Wicked people don't have strong roots. They can easily be demolished. [Proverbs 10:30]

Reader: Why is it so important that I work on my speech and how I talk to people?
Answer: Words are powerful. They can encourage people and help them get through difficult situations. [Proverbs 10:31-32]

Proverbs 11

Reader: Does God care how people do business deals?
Answer: God wants you to be fair when doing business deals. He hates it when people get cheated out of money and scammed. [Proverbs 11:1]

Reader: Why do people get fired from their jobs?
Answer: They're prideful. They feel they can treat their coworkers however they want to. People who are wise show their coworkers respect. [Proverbs 11:2]

Reader: What is a red flag that the person I'm dating is not marriage material?
Answer: They are dishonest and lie to you all the time. You want to marry someone honest and trustworthy. [Proverbs 11:3]

Reader: Can you buy your way into heaven?
Answer: No, you have to live a godly life. [Proverbs 11:4]

Reader: What directs godly people?

Answer: Their honesty. [Proverbs 11:5]

Reader: What happens to people who are not honest?
Answer: The sin they commit will eventually destroy them. [Proverbs 11:5]

Reader: Is there anything wrong with being ambitious and wanting to be successful?
Answer: There is nothing wrong with wanting to be successful. It's just that too many people want financial success over spiritual success. Focus on being spiritually successful and living a life that pleases God, and over time, God will make you financially successful as well. [Proverbs 11:6]

Reader: What happens when wicked people die?
Answer: All of their hopes and dreams die with them. They won't be remembered because they gave credit to themselves for their success instead of God. [Proverbs 11:7]

Reader: What advantage do godly people have over the wicked?

Answer: God protects those who love Him from trouble and it falls on the wicked instead. [Proverbs 11:8]

Reader: What is the most powerful weapon on the face of the earth?
Answer: Believe it or not it's your tongue. Your words can destroy relationships like a fire that destroys a house, but if you use your words wisely you can save people's lives like a fireman.
[Proverbs 11:9]

Reader: When godly people are in positions of power how do people feel about it?
Answer: They rejoice because they know that their power won't go to their head and corrupt them.
[Proverbs 11:10-11]

Reader: Should I slander people I know that have done me wrong?
Answer: Don't speak evil of them. God knows what they've done. Let Him handle the matter. [Proverbs 11:12]

Reader: If someone tells me something confidential what should I do?
Answer: The person that told you the information trusts you. Don't tell their business to others. Keep their information private. [Proverbs 11:13]

Reader: What is the key to having a great government?
Answer: Having wise leaders with good advisors that can give them honest and trustworthy advice. [Proverbs 11:14]

Reader: If someone is constantly asking me to help them with their bills what should I do?
Answer: Tell them no. If you're always paying their bills they will never learn how to budget their money. [Proverbs 11:15]

Reader: Do violent men get respect?
Answer: No, the only thing they get is wealth from the crimes they commit. [Proverbs 11:16]

Reader: Can being kind benefit me?
Answer: Yes, being kind to people will help you gain honor and respect. Being cruel will cause

people to despise you and not want to be around you. [Proverbs 11:17]

Reader: What happens to people who get rich from scams?
Answer: Their money won't last. [Proverbs 11:18]

Reader: What about godly people who get rich?
Answer: Their money will last for their entire life time. [Proverbs 11:18]

Reader: If you're determined to live a godly life, what will happen?
Answer: You will go to heaven. [Proverbs 11:19]

Reader: What about people who are determined to live an evil life?
Answer: They will end up in hell. [Proverbs 11:19]

Reader: Does God like people who live double lives?
Answer: No, He hates it. But He loves people who have integrity. [Proverbs 11:20]

Reader: Will God punish those who are evil?

Answer: Yes, but the godly will be blessed and their children too. [Proverbs 11:21]

Reader: What should I look for in a future wife?
Answer: Make sure she's wise. If she's beautiful but lacks common sense the relationship won't last. [Proverbs 11:22]

Reader: What kind of reward can a godly person expect?
Answer: They can expect earthly and heavenly blessings. [Proverbs 11:23]

Reader: What about the wicked?
Answer: The only thing they can expect is God's judgment. [Proverbs 11:23]

Reader: If I want to increase my wealth what should I do?
Answer: Give to people in need. If you're stingy with your money you'll eventually lose it. Be generous with your wealth and you'll prosper. When you help others in their time of need God will see to it that you receive help when you need it. [Proverbs 11:24-25]

Reader: Should business owners lower their prices in a recession?

Answer: Yes. Some businesses raise their prices and try to take advantage of a bad economy. Godly business owners lower their prices to help those who are struggling financially. [Proverbs 11:26]

Reader: If I try to find ways to do evil to others what'll happen?

Answer: Evil will come to you instead. [Proverbs 11:27]

Reader: If I try to find ways to do good to others what'll happen?

Answer: The favor of God will be on your life. [Proverbs 11:27]

Reader: Why do some people lose all their money and go bankrupt?

Answer: They trusted in their money instead of God. The godly realize that their wealth is a gift from God and use it to help others. They will prosper like trees in spring. [Proverbs 11:28]

Reader: How can I prevent my family from falling apart?

Answer: Treat your spouse and children with respect. [Proverbs 11:29]

Reader: Why do some people have more friends than others?
Answer: They treat people how they want to be treated. [Proverbs 11:30]

Reader: Do I have to wait until I get to heaven to get rewarded for being good?
Answer: No, God can reward you while on earth, but He will punish the wicked. [Proverbs 11:31]

Proverbs 12

Reader: How can I be more disciplined?
Answer: To develop discipline you must be willing to learn from others. [Proverbs 12:1]

Reader: What kind of people does God approve of?
Answer: Those who try to obey Him. He disapproves of people who plan to commit sin. [Proverbs 12:2]

Reader: Why is it that some countries don't have stable governments?
Answer: The people in charge are wicked. The best leaders are the ones that have a stable relationship with God. [Proverbs 12:3]

Reader: How important is it that I choose a good wife?
Answer: Very important! Your wife can tear you down or she can build you up. The woman you choose to marry should make you feel like a king, not a slave. [Proverbs 12:4]

Reader: How can I know if someone can be trusted?

Answer: They're reliable. They also give you good advice. [Proverbs 12:5]

Reader: Is it possible to murder someone without physically killing them?
Answer: Yes. People murder people every day with the words they say. [Proverbs 12:6]

Reader: What happens when an evil person dies?
Answer: Their families never think about them again. [Proverbs 12:7]

Reader: What about when godly people die?
Answer: Their legacy will continue to go forth many generations after their death. [Proverbs 12:7]

Reader: Should I strive to be intelligent?
Answer: Yes. The more knowledge you have the more respect you receive from others. If you don't seek knowledge no one will listen to what you have to say. [Proverbs 12:8]

Reader: Is there anything wrong with wanting to be popular?

Answer: People who try to act important don't get anywhere in life. They deceive themselves. It's better to be yourself. [Proverbs 12:9]

Reader: Can you find out a person's character by how they treat their pet?
Answer: If they treat their animals maliciously then they'll treat people the same way. Godly people are concerned about the welfare of their pets just like they're concerned about the welfare of people. [Proverbs 12:10]

Reader: What do women appreciate about a hardworking man?
Answer: Their willingness to work to provide for his family. When a woman has a man that's not lazy and wants to provide for the needs of his family she will respect him. [Proverbs 12:11]

Reader: Is it wrong to invest in a business deal that will make me a lot of money fast?
Answer: Stay away from quick money schemes and earn your money legally. You will prosper if you do. [Proverbs 12:12]

Reader: How do people trap themselves with their own words?

Answer: When they get caught in a lie. Godly people don't have to worry about that because they're honest and truthful. [Proverbs 12:13]

Reader: What are some things I can do to be successful in the work force?

Answer: Use your words and hands wisely. Having good speech and a good work ethic will take you to the top of any company. [Proverbs 12:14]

Reader: Should I get my wife's advice before making a decision?

Answer: Some husbands think they know everything and never consult their wives. A wise husband will always seek to know what his wife thinks before making a final decision. [Proverbs 12:15]

Reader: What's the best way to respond to an insult?

Answer: Seal your lips like a Ziploc bag. The best response is no response at all. [Proverbs 12:16]

Reader: Why is it that some people are not found guilty for the crime they committed?
Answer: The witness told a lie. An honest witness will tell the truth. [Proverbs 12:17]

Reader: Some people say that the tongue can be compared to a knife. How so?
Answer: Words cut people and hurt them. When you say things like, "I hate you," you can really wound a person. When you say, "I love you," you heal the person. [Proverbs 12:18]

Reader: If someone lies on me what should I do?
Answer: Wait it out. God will expose the person who told the lie. [Proverbs 12:19]

Reader: Can you tell if a person is planning to do good or evil?
Answer: You can't see what they're thinking, but what you can see is their actions. Watching someone's behavior will let you know all about them. [Proverbs 12:20]

Reader: What's a sign that someone is evil?

Answer: They have no peace and are suspicious of everyone. A godly person's life is peaceful. [Proverbs 12:21]

Reader: Is there anything wrong with breaking a promise?
Answer: Breaking a promise is the same thing as telling a lie. If you break a promise you made the best thing for you to do is tell the person that you made the agreement with the truth of why you broke the promise and apologize to them. [Proverbs 12:22]

Reader: Should I brag about how much knowledge I have?
Answer: Never brag on how smart you are, only fools do that. There's always someone that has more knowledge and wisdom than you do. [Proverbs 12:23]

Reader: What happens to people who refuse to work and make a living?
Answer: They'll end up becoming slaves to bill collectors and be in debt because they're too lazy to find employment. [Proverbs 12:24]

Reader: If my wife is worried about a situation how can I cheer her up?
Answer: Be compassionate towards her and listen to what she has to say. By doing this you will encourage her and make her feel better. [Proverbs 12:25]

Reader: Is it wise to give someone advice I wouldn't take myself?
Answer. No. You will cause more harm than good. When giving advice ask yourself what would God do. [Proverbs 12:26]

Reader: What should I do if I have left over food?
Answer: Lazy people let food spoil and go to waste. Wise people don't. If they have left over food they give it to someone who needs it. [Proverbs 12:27]

Reader: What's the greatest decision a person can make?
Answer: To give their life to Christ. In life there are two paths, one that leads to heaven and the other that leads to hell. You get to decide which path you choose. [Proverbs 12:28]

Proverbs 13

Reader: Why are some children better behaved than others?
Answer: Their parents refuse to discipline them. That's why you see kids running around in stores tearing up the place. Children that are disciplined obey their parents at home and in public. [Proverbs 13:1]

Reader: What is having a good conversation like?
Answer: It's like eating at a five-star restaurant. [Proverbs 13:2]

Reader: How can I keep myself out of danger when talking to someone?
Answer: Watch what you say. It's easy to get yourself in an argument. Once you say something you can never get those words back. [Proverbs 13:3]

Reader: What do lazy people like to do with their time?
Answer: Daydream about the future. Hard workers don't do that. They work diligently to make their dream a reality. [Proverbs 13:4]

Reader: What can tarnish a person's reputation?
Answer: Telling a lie on them that's not true.
[Proverbs 13:5]

Reader: What's the purpose of memorizing the Bible?
Answer: So you'll know what to do when you're faced with a dilemma. [Proverbs 13:6]

Reader: They say that looks can be deceiving. Is this true?
Answer: Some people want you to think they're rich so they go buy fancy clothes, expensive cars, and lavish houses. On the other hand, some people pretend they don't have a dime and have millions in their bank account. [Proverbs 13:7]

Reader: Is there an advantage to being poor?
Answer: Poor people don't have to worry about being extorted or robbed because they don't have money. People try to blackmail rich people all the time. [Proverbs 13:8]

Reader: What is light a symbol of?

Answer: A good life. The opposite is darkness. It represents people who live an evil life. [Proverbs 13:9]

Reader: How can I know if someone is prideful?
Answer: They argue with a person trying to give them advice. [Proverbs 13:10]

Reader: How is it that some people get rich over night?
Answer: They invested their money in a get-rich-quick scheme. The money they acquire won't last. People who work hard and earn an honest living, their money will increase over time. [Proverbs 13:11]

Reader: How am I supposed to feel if I'm looking forward to something that hasn't happened in my life yet?
Answer: Don't give up hope. Wait expectantly on God to make your dream come true. [Proverbs 13:12]

Reader: Should I seek advice from people at work?
Answer: Yes. Being a team player is the key to being successful at work. Your co-workers will

respect you more by asking them for their advice and input. [Proverbs 13:13]

Reader: What can bring down your ministry the fastest?
Answer: Having the mentality that everything depends on you for your ministry to be successful. When you're in ministry you need to allow others to give you input and suggestions so that your ministry can thrive and grow. [Proverbs 13:14]

Reader: Why is it that some people are more respected than others?
Answer: People who are honest and trustworthy get more respect than people who tell lies. [Proverbs 13:15]

Reader: What should I do before I make a decision?
Answer: In order to make the best decision possible you need to think about the negative and positive consequences. Fools don't think before they make their decisions. They even have the audacity to brag about it. [Proverbs 13:16]

Reader: Does the Bible mention anything about text messaging?

Answer: Not specifically, but a good rule of thumb is when you text someone a message make sure that it doesn't hurt their feelings. [Proverbs 13:17]

Reader: Why?
Answer: Because they can go back and look at the message over and over again. It'll be harder for them to erase it out of their mind. When you text make sure it's uplifting and encouraging. If you have to talk about something of importance have a phone conversation or talk to them in person. [Proverbs 13:17]

Reader: Is it wise to get advice before making big financial decisions?
Answer: Yes. A lot of men and women have made bad financial decisions because they didn't seek out advice before making the purchase. God honors people who get advice from others. [Proverbs 13:18]

Reader: Why do some people never achieve their dreams?
Answer: They have a particular sin or sins in their life they're not willing to give up. [Proverbs 13:19]

Reader: I have a dream of getting married one day and having a family. Is there anything I can do now to prepare?
Answer: Talk to married couples and get advice from them. [Proverbs 13:20]

Reader: What happens to people who sin all the time?
Answer: They attract trouble. [Proverbs 13:21]

Reader: What about the godly?
Answer: The godly attract God's blessings as a reward for doing what pleases Him. [Proverbs 13:21]

Reader: What happens to the money of a godly person after they die?
Answer: The money is passed on to their grandkids. [Proverbs 13:22]

Reader: What happens to the money of a person who is wicked after they die?
Answer: Their money will be given to the godly. [Proverbs 13:22]

Reader: Why is it that some people are poor after spending most of their life working hard to earn an honest living?

Answer: Two things may have occurred. They could have made a bad financial decision that caused them to lose their money, or they could have lost their health which caused them not to be able to work anymore. [Proverbs 13:23]

Reader: How can I show my child that I love them?
Answer: Punish them when they disobey you.
[Proverbs 13:24]

Reader: Are wicked people ever satisfied?
Answer: They always want more. The godly are satisfied. That's why God blesses them with more.
[Proverbs 13:25]

Proverbs 14

Reader: How can a wife destroy her family?
Answer: By the way she talks to her husband and children. A wise wife will build her family up with her words. A foolish wife will tear hers down.
[Proverbs 14:1]

Reader: How can I show God that I respect Him?
Answer: By living the way you should. Living a sinful lifestyle shows that you have no respect for God.
[Proverbs 14:2]

Reader: They say sticks and stones break bones, but words will never hurt you. Is this true?
Answer: In some cases, words hurt worse than breaking an arm or leg. After a surgery or an injury there will be a permanent scar. The same can be said for words. They leave emotional scars.
[Proverbs 14:3]

Reader: What should I do if I have a large project to complete in a short period of time?
Answer: Ask for help. By asking for help you'll make sure the project gets done properly and on time. By not asking for help you risk the chance of the

project being late and not done properly. [Proverbs 14:4]

Reader: What do lawyers need to realize about their line of work?
Answer: Some witnesses tell lies and others tell the truth. [Proverbs 14:5]

Reader: What's the difference between a close-minded person and an opened-minded person?
Answer: Open-minded people are open to receive counsel. Close-minded people think that their way is right and yours is wrong. They hate advice. [Proverbs 14:6]

Reader: How can I avoid wasting time?
Answer: Have a schedule and stick to it. [Proverbs 14:7]

Reader: What can prevent me from reaching a goal?
Answer: Distractions. Distractions kill dreams. Being focused will bring your dreams to life. [Proverbs 14:8]

Reader: If I know I've wronged someone what should I do?
Answer: Seek reconciliation. The more time you wait to apologize the harder it will be for the person to forgive you. [Proverbs 14:9]

Reader: If a friend is going through a difficult time what should I do?
Answer: Don't shy away from them. Do everything you can to encourage them and lift their spirits. [Proverbs 14:10]

Reader: If all a person has to live in is a tent how should they feel?
Answer: Living in a tent with the protection and favor of God is better than living in a mansion with God as your enemy. [Proverbs 14:11]

Reader: What can kill a person's life the quickest?
Answer: Things that seem harmless and insignificant. For example, a married man having lunch with his secretary once or twice a week seems harmless, but what started out as just having lunch will turn into an affair destroying his family. [Proverbs 14:12]

Reader: Is it a good idea to hide my emotions?
Answer: Some people smile during the day and cry themselves to sleep at night. If you're going through a difficult time reach out to a family member or a friend for support. [Proverbs 14:13]

Reader: What is the reward for being consistent?
Answer: Your life will move forward instead of backwards. Life is all about progress and growth. If you want results, be consistent at whatever you're attempting to do. [Proverbs 14:14]

Reader: How can I know if a woman is wise?
Answer: She won't believe everything a man tells her. Some men tell women lies and flatter them just so they can sleep with them. A wise woman will see right through their lies and deception. [Proverbs 14:15]

Reader: Is there anything wrong with being overly cautious?
Answer: No there is not. Being cautious with your words and actions can keep you out of trouble. Fools are reckless. They don't think before they do anything. [Proverbs 14:16]

Reader: Why do fools have quick tempers?
Answer: They lack self-control. They have a hard time controlling their emotions. That's why people hate being around them. [Proverbs 14:17]

Reader: Why is having knowledge considered to be a reward from God?
Answer: Because you will have the wisdom necessary to be successful in every area of your life. [Proverbs 14:18]

Reader: If a person doesn't respect me what should I do?
Answer: Don't worry about it. Eventually they won't have a choice because of your influence and character. [Proverbs 14:19]

Reader: Why do poor people not have friends?
Answer: Because of their lack of money. Rich people have lots of friends because of their wealth. [Proverbs 14:20]

Reader: Should I talk bad about people that I see regularly?

Answer: No. Eventually they will find out and be upset with you for talking behind their back. [Proverbs 14:21]

Reader: Will helping someone out that is poor benefit me?
Answer: Yes, it will! God will bless you for your kindness. [Proverbs 14:22]

Reader: How can I gain the respect and loyalty of someone I don't know?
Answer: Ask them questions. By doing this you will show them that you're interested in getting to know them and becoming their friend. [Proverbs 14:22]

Reader: Why do some people struggle to make a living?
Answer: They like to talk more than they like to work. There is nothing wrong with talking about your future plans and goals, but if you don't roll up your sleeves and get to work you'll end up broke. [Proverbs 14:23]

Reader: What happens when a person makes wise decisions with their money?

Answer: Their money accumulates and they can achieve financial freedom. Fools are always lacking financially because they spend their money irresponsibly. [Proverbs 14:24]

Reader: How important is it that a jury is selected carefully?
Answer: They hold the life of the person that is on trial in the palm of their hands. They can sentence them to go to prison for the rest of their life, or they can let them go free. [Proverbs 14:25]

Reader: If I respect God while I'm living what will happen when I die?
Answer: God will look out for your children after you're gone. [Proverbs 14:26]

Reader: What else can respecting God do for me?
Answer: It will prevent you from doing things outside of God's will that could harm you. [Proverbs 14:27]

Reader: What is a sign that a leader of a nation is losing power?
Answer: The people they're over refuse to follow them anymore. [Proverbs 14:28]

Reader: Is there anything wrong with being angry?
Answer: No, the problem occurs when you allow your anger to get the best of you and you lash out at the person who upset you. [Proverbs 14:29]

Reader: Can being jealous affect my health?
Answer: Jealousy is like cancer; it can start off small and grows rapidly if it isn't dealt with. [Proverbs 14:30]

Reader: Is it possible to insult God?
Answer: Yes, if you mistreat the poor. You can honor God by helping them. [Proverbs 14:31]

Reader: If a wicked person faces a crisis what will happen to them?
Answer: They won't be able to survive it. The godly will be able to handle anything life throws their way because God will keep them safe. [Proverbs 14:32]

Reader: What do wise people think about during the day?
Answer: Trying to please God. [Proverbs 14:33]

Reader: What do wicked people think about during the day?
Answer: What kind of sins they are going to commit later. [Proverbs 14:33]

Reader: How can a nation go from being awful to great?
Answer: Having leaders that love God and hate sin. [Proverbs 14:34]

Reader: What can make a leader rejoice?
Answer: When the people he or she is over is just as wise as they are. [Proverbs 14:35]

Reader: What can make a leader angry?
Answer: When the people they are over turn their backs on them. [Proverbs 14:35]

Proverbs 15

Reader: What is the best way to stop an argument before it gets out of control?
Answer: Watch the tone of your voice. When people argue they normally yell. Speak softly to get your point across. [Proverbs 15:1]

Reader: What should a good pastor be able to do?
Answer: Preach sermons that inspire people to live a godly life. [Proverbs 15:2]

Reader: Is there anything God doesn't know about?
Answer: No. He knows everything good and evil people do. [Proverbs 15:3]

Reader: If someone has been verbally abused how can I help them overcome it?
Answer: Speak positive about them and express your love for them verbally. [Proverbs 15:4]

Reader: What do children need the most when they're young?
Answer: Discipline from their parents. If a child is never disciplined they won't be able to become wise. [Proverbs 15:5]

Reader: What do godly people have in their house that evil people don't?
Answer: Peace. Peace is one of the greatest treasures a family can possess. Evil people don't have peace in their homes. There is always turmoil. [Proverbs 15:6]

Reader: If someone asks me to give them advice and I don't know what to tell them, what should I do?
Answer: Point them toward a person that can give them the advice they need. [Proverbs 15:7]

Reader: Does prayer really work?
Answer: If you pretend to be godly, God won't hear your prayers, but if you practice what you preach, God will hear every word you pray to Him. [Proverbs 15:8]

Reader: How does God feel about people who live in sin and refuse to change?
Answer: It breaks His heart and angers Him. [Proverbs 15:9]

Reader: How does He feel about people who decide to change and live for Him?
Answer: It brings Him great happiness and joy. [Proverbs 15:9]

Reader: How does God punish people who don't like being corrected?
Answer: He allows them to experience frustration in the area they refuse to be corrected in. [Proverbs 15:10]

Reader: Is there anything I can hide from God?
Answer: There is nothing you can hide from God. If He knows what is going on in heaven and hell surely, He knows what's going on in your mind. [Proverbs 15:11]

Reader: Why do foolish people avoid the wise?
Answer: They are afraid their secret sins will be exposed. [Proverbs 15:12]

Reader: How can I tell if someone is going through a trial?
Answer: The look on their face will tell it all. A person's body language can tell you how they are feeling inside. [Proverbs 15:13]

Reader: Should I read gossip?
Answer: Don't feed your mind trash. Instead, read books that will strengthen your mind. [Proverbs 15:14]

Reader: Is there such a thing as bad luck?
Answer: Foolish people sin and when their life falls apart they say they've got bad luck. Wise people don't believe in bad luck because they realize that God's favor is on their life. [Proverbs 15:15]

Reader: Why are some celebrities unhappy?
Answer: They love success more than they love God. [Proverbs 15:16]

Reader: What is better than eating at a five-star restaurant?
Answer: Sharing a pizza at home with people that love you unconditionally. [Proverbs 15:17]

Reader: How can I control the atmosphere in my home?
Answer: Control your temper. [Proverbs 15:18]

Reader: Can a person block their own blessings?

Answer: If they are lazy they can. If they are diligent and consistent they'll be blessed with success. [Proverbs 15:19]

Reader: What causes godly parents grief and pain?
Answer: A foolish child that doesn't respect God. [Proverbs 15:20]

Reader: Why do fools enjoy sinning so much?
Answer: To them sinning is fun. Godly men and women hate sinning because they know it hurts God. [Proverbs 15:21]

Reader: Before I attempt any new endeavor, what should I do first?
Answer: Get advice from a trusted friend or family member whether you should do it or not. [Proverbs 15:22]

Reader: What is a benefit of reading the Bible?
Answer: When someone you know is in a crisis you will be able to give them scripture on how to overcome it. [Proverbs 15:23]

Reader: What is the final destination for the wise?

Answer: Heaven, they have no fear of going to hell. [Proverbs 15:24]

Reader: What happens to the household of a prideful husband?
Answer: His house will fall apart because he refuses to listen to his wife and insist on doing things his way. [Proverbs 15:25]

Reader: What irritates God?
Answer: Husbands that fantasize about being with other women instead of their wives. [Proverbs 15:26]

Reader: What excites Him?
Answer: Husbands that praise and cherish their wives. [Proverbs 15:26]

Reader: Can finances ruin a marriage?
Answer: Yes. If your spouse is making money illegally it will devastate not only you but your children's future. [Proverbs 15:27]

Reader: Why do so many couples get into arguments?

Answer: They don't think before they speak. [Proverbs 15:28]

Reader: What can I do to ensure that God hears my prayers?
Answer: Try your best to live a life of integrity. If you have hidden sins in your life God will ignore you when you pray to Him. [Proverbs 15:29]

Reader: What is a good habit to develop before I get married?
Answer: Controlling your facial expressions. When you look down and out your spouse will pick up on it and think that you are mad at them. [Proverbs 15:30]

Reader: Is being wise hard?
Answer: Sometimes it can be because in order to become wise you have to accept constructive criticism. [Proverbs 15:31-32]

Reader: How can I show God that I respect Him?
Answer: Kill your pride and realize that God knows more about life than you do. [Proverbs 15:33]

Proverbs 16

Reader: Is it good for people to make plans for the future?
Answer: You can make plans. Just remember that God can change them if He wants to. [Proverbs 16:1]

Reader: Why shouldn't I judge people?
Answer: Because you have flaws yourself. Even though people can't see your flaws God knows all about them. [Proverbs 16:2]

Reader: I'm working at a job I don't like. What should I do?
Answer: Do something every day that will put you in position to do what you love. That way when the opportunity comes you can leave your current job for your dream job. [Proverbs 16:3]

Reader: Why did God create hell?
Answer: To punish the wicked. [Proverbs 16:4]

Reader: Are there repercussions for being arrogant?

Answer: God doesn't like people who are arrogant. It's better to be humble so you won't have to face the wrath of God. [Proverbs 16:5]

Reader: If I feel guilty after I do something I'm not supposed to what should I do?
Answer: Ask God for forgiveness and He'll forgive your sins. [Proverbs 16:6]

Reader: What does fearing God do?
Answer: It helps you avoid sinning against Him. [Proverbs 16:6]

Reader: Should I worry about my enemies?
Answer: If your life is pleasing to God you won't have to worry about your enemies. They will be at peace with you. [Proverbs 16:7]

Reader: Should I strive to be rich?
Answer: There is nothing wrong with wanting to be rich, just don't earn your money illegally.
It's better to be honest and not make a lot of money than to be rich and corrupt. [Proverbs 16:8]

Reader: I've made my plans for the future. What should I do now?

Answer: Be flexible. God might bring your dream to pass in a way you never expected. [Proverbs 16:9]

Reader: What does a good leader have to be able to do?
Answer: They should speak to the people they are leading with respect and be a good judge of character. [Proverbs 16:10]

Reader: What does God think of managers who cheat their employees?
Answer: He hates it. He wants them to treat their employees fairly and not take advantage of them. [Proverbs 16:11]

Reader: How can we improve the government?
Answer: Vote for leaders that stand for justice and hate evil. [Proverbs 16:12]

Reader: What can I do to please a person in authority?
Answer: Be honest and truthful with your actions and words. [Proverbs 16:13]

Reader: If my boss gets upset what can I do to calm them down?

Answer: Give them time to cool off. Don't try to talk to them right away because they won't hear a word you say. After they've cooled off approach them and find out if you can do anything to make them feel better. [Proverbs 16:14]

Reader: What does working for an incredible boss feel like?
Answer: It's like a nice cool rain on a spring day. It's wonderful. [Proverbs 16:15]

Reader: What is better than being a millionaire?
Answer: Having wisdom. Wisdom will give you peace, honor, and the ability to make tough decisions easily. These are things money can't buy. [Proverbs 16:16]

Reader: When making a decision what should I think about?
Answer: You should think about whether or not the decision is going to cause you or someone else to sin. [Proverbs 16:17]

Reader: What is a sign that a person is prideful?
Answer: They think they are better than you are. [Proverbs 16:18]

Reader: What is something rich people must watch out for?
Answer: Becoming stingy. Try your best to share your money with people in need. [Proverbs 16:19]

Reader: Is going to college a good decision?
Answer: Yes, if you plan on listening to what your instructors teach you. [Proverbs 16:20]

Reader: While attending college what should I remember to do?
Answer: There is going to be a lot of distractions pulling at you while in college. Trust God and do the right thing and you will have a great college experience. [Proverbs 16:20]

Reader: What are wise people known for?
Answer: They are known for being understanding and considerate toward others. They also have the ability to persuade others to obey God's Word. [Proverbs 16:21]

Reader: If a person doesn't have the discipline to learn God's Word what will happen to them?

Answer: When they are tempted to sin or have an important decision to make they won't know what to do. [Proverbs 16:22]

Reader: How can I tell if someone is intelligent?
Answer: The words they speak are wise and believable. [Proverbs 16:23]

Reader: Can the words you hear daily affect your health?
Answer: Yes. If a person is being verbally abused they will experience depression and have high blood pressure from stress. If someone is in a healthy loving relationship they will be more energetic and full of life. [Proverbs 16:24]

Reader: How do you know if you're addicted to something?
Answer: You've tried to stop, but you don't have the power to. [Proverbs 16:25]

Reader: What will drive people to work harder and get more production from them?
Answer: Not eating until the job gets done. There's nothing like a good meal after a hard day's work. [Proverbs 16:26]

Reader: What is similar to a wildfire?
Answer: A person with a wild tongue. Their speech can cause a lot of damage in a short amount of time. [Proverbs 16:27]

Reader: Some people can be friends for years then overnight they hate each other. What happened to ruin their friendship so quickly?
Answer: Gossip. More than likely one of the friends has been gossiping behind the other person's back and their friend has found out about it from someone else. [Proverbs 16:28]

Reader: Why do people join gangs?
Answer: The leaders of the gang make them feel accepted and loved. [Proverbs 16:29]

Reader: How can I tell if a person is a con artist?
Answer: By looking at their face. They have a sneaky smile and wink a lot. [Proverbs 16:30]

Reader: Is having gray hair a bad thing?
Answer: No, it means you've lived a godly life. [Proverbs 16:31]

Reader: What's better than conquering a city?

Answer: Being patient and having self-control. If you can control your emotions you can control everything else in your life. [Proverbs 16:32]

Reader: Just because I make plans does God have to make them come to pass?
Answer: If your plans please God He will make them come to pass, but if your plans are not in His will it won't happen. [Proverbs 16:33]

Reader: Should I stop making plans?
Answer: It's okay to make plans, but remember that God's plans for your life are better than yours. [Proverbs 16:33]

Proverbs 17

Reader: What is better than eating out?
Answer: Your house not being full of drama and conflict. When there is strife in your home you're too angry to think about food. [Proverbs 17:1]

Reader: What is the difference between a person who grew up in privilege and one who didn't?
Answer: Children who grow up in households where they didn't have to work to earn their success don't know what hard work is like. Children who become successful starting from nothing know what it means to work hard. [Proverbs 17:2]

Reader: What can a person do to break a pornography addiction?
Answer: When you purify something, you use fire. Breaking a pornography addiction is like having your flesh set on fire; it's going to be very painful at first, but the pain will eventually turn into power so that you will be able to resist watching it. [Proverbs 17:3]

Reader: Is there anything wrong with listening to gossip?

Answer: The more you listen to gossip the more you will become addicted to listening to it and eventually you will start gossiping about others. [Proverbs 17:4]

Reader: What will happen if someone makes fun of a poor person?
Answer: God will punish them. Making fun of poor people insults God. [Proverbs 17:5]

Reader: What is the best thing about being old?
Answer: Having grandkids to play with. [Proverbs 17:6]

Reader: How do foolish people try to impress people?
Answer: They try to use articulate and eloquent words to make themselves sound smart when they're really not. [Proverbs 17:7]

Reader: Why is it that people get placed in positions of power and they are not qualified to do the job?
Answer: More than likely they bribed somebody to get the position. [Proverbs 17:8]

Reader: If my spouse and I are mad at each other what should I do?

Answer: Resolve the issue as quickly as possible. Never go to bed mad at each other. Showing love will bring you back together; being hateful will separate the two of you. [Proverbs 17:9]

Reader: How come foolish people don't learn from their mistakes?

Answer: They don't want to learn and they like living in sin. Wise people hate sin and will ask for advice on how to avoid it. [Proverbs 17:10]

Reader: Is it smart to rebel against the person who supervises you?

Answer: Fighting with your boss is never a smart thing to do; you're asking to be fired. [Proverbs 17:11]

Reader: When foolish people get caught doing something wrong what should I do?

Answer: Don't try to get them to admit what they did was wrong. They will call you a liar and try to slander your name. [Proverbs 17:12]

Reader: If my spouse is good to me, but I treat them badly, what will happen?
Answer: God will punish you until you repent and change your ways. [Proverbs 17:13]

Reader: If I can tell I'm about to get into an argument with someone what's the best thing for me to do?
Answer: Stopping yourself from saying what is on your mind is difficult, but it'll save you a lot of heart ache and pain. [Proverbs 17:14]

Reader: What does God hate most about the judicial system?
Answer: People who let the guilty go free and lock the innocent up. [Proverbs 17:15]

Reader: Is there anything wrong with a person wanting to go to college?
Answer: Some kids just want to go to college to party and have fun, but they end up flunking out of school wasting their parents' money. [Proverbs 17:16]

Reader: What can I do to show my girlfriend I'm serious about marrying her one day?

Answer: Be loyal to her. If she knows that you're faithful to her and not cheating on her it will give her the emotional security she needs and desires. [Proverbs 17:17]

Reader: If a friend needs a loan from me, should I do it?
Answer: Never take out a loan for a friend. You put your credit at risk. Once your credit is ruined it can be hard to build it back up again. [Proverbs 17:18]

Reader: When people come to me and want to vent about an argument they got into should I listen to them?
Answer: Be cautious. They might be trying to play the victim. If they always blame the other person and don't take responsibility for their part in the argument they may be trying to sway you to take their side. [Proverbs 17:19]

Reader: Is it good to brag on what you have in your home?
Answer: No, because the person listening to you might try to rob you. [Proverbs 17:19]

Reader: What will happen to a person who is crooked and takes advantage of people?
Answer: The same trouble they caused to their victims will come right back to them ten times worse. [Proverbs 17:20]

Reader: How serious is it that I raise my kids the right way?
Answer: If you don't, they will rebel when they get older and cause you grief and pain. [Proverbs 17:21]

Reader: How can I help cheer someone up who is going through a hard time?
Answer: Take them to dinner. A good meal and a great conversation is the best medicine to help them feel better. [Proverbs 17:22]

Reader: If a person gets acquitted of a crime they committed what has happened?
Answer: Either the judge or several jurors have been bribed and paid off. [Proverbs 17:23]

Reader: What should I focus my attention on every day?

Answer: Seeking wisdom. Seeking wisdom will help you grow. Fools don't focus on anything but sinning, that's why their lives are always in turmoil. [Proverbs 17:24]

Reader: If a child is in and out of jail, should their parents come to their rescue?
Answer: No, they need to learn from their mistakes. If you keep bailing them out, they will keep getting in trouble. [Proverbs 17:25]

Reader: How come good leaders don't speak their minds sometimes?
Answer: They are afraid they will be ridiculed for speaking the truth. [Proverbs 17:26]

Reader: What do wise people do differently than foolish people?
Answer: Wise people know how to control their emotions, fools don't. [Proverbs 17:27]

Reader: How can I learn to control my emotions?
Answer: Don't talk a lot. There is nothing wrong with being quiet sometimes. It will keep you out of trouble. Even foolish people can look wise when they keep their mouths shut. [Proverbs 17:28]

Proverbs 18

Reader: Should I try to give someone advice that likes to do things their own way?
Answer: No, don't do it. They will lash out at you for trying to help them. [Proverbs 18:1]

Reader: Is it okay to give my opinion when having a discussion?
Answer: There is nothing wrong with expressing how you feel, the problem occurs when you try to force your opinion on someone else. [Proverbs 18:2]

Reader: How do people get themselves caught up in scandals?
Answer: They commit secret sins that no one knows about and try to lie to cover their tracks. [Proverbs 18:3]

Reader: What trait does a good teacher have?
Answer: They speak with wisdom. A student will enjoy coming to class if he or she knows their teacher is going to pour knowledge and wisdom into them. [Proverbs 18:4]

Reader: Is it important that a person get a fair trial?
Answer: Yes, there's a lot at stake. If a person is found guilty of a crime they didn't commit, they may never see their family again. If a guilty person is found innocent they may commit the same crime over again. [Proverbs 18:5]

Reader: What is a characteristic of someone that's immature?
Answer: They love to get into arguments with people. They love the thrill of getting someone mad by what they say. [Proverbs 18:6]

Reader: Will they ever learn?
Answer: They won't learn until their life gets threatened by the person they have upset. [Proverbs 18:7]

Reader: Why should I stay away from gossiping about people?
Answer: The more you gossip the more enemies you'll have. People don't like to be talked about behind their back. [Proverbs 18:8]

Reader: Can being lazy at work hurt the company I work for?

Answer: If you're lazy at work you will hurt the production of your co-workers and fellow employees. Your laziness will affect their job performance as well as yours. [Proverbs 18:9]

Reader: Can money protect you?
Answer: People think their money will protect them when they get caught in a jam, godly people don't trust in their money to protect them, they trust in God. [Proverbs 18:10]

Reader: Some people I know are stuck on themselves and arrogant.
Answer: Don't worry about it, God will bring them down to reality. [Proverbs 18:11]

Reader: What about the humble?
Answer: God will honor them. [Proverbs 18:12]

Reader: When my wife talks to me about a situation that happened at work should I offer her advice.
Answer: Not until after you've listened to what she's had to say first. A lot of times women don't want an answer or a solution to fix their problem,

they just want you to console them and listen.
[Proverbs 18:13]

Reader: I'm having a really hard time recovering from a break up.
Answer: The death of a relationship can be painful, but remember that after there's a death there will always be a resurrection. God will resurrect you and bring someone special into your life to date.
[Proverbs 18:14]

Reader: What's the key to enjoying the Bible?
Answer: Having the right attitude. Most people read the Bible with an "I have to" attitude. God wants you to read the Bible with an "I want to" attitude. [Proverbs 18:15]

Reader: Is there anything wrong with giving someone an unexpected gift?
Answer: If your motives are right. Sometimes gifts are used to bribe people. [Proverbs 18:16]

Reader: Is it right to make a decision before hearing both sides of the story?
Answer: It's easy to make decisions based on emotion. Don't be in a hurry, get all the

information you need first then make a decision.
[Proverbs 18:17]

Reader: How do people who don't know God make tough decisions?
Answer: They flip a coin to decide what to do.
[Proverbs 18:18]

Reader: Why is it good that I don't get into arguments with my spouse?
Answer: The more arguments you get in the further apart you become. It's hard trying to get your spouse to love you if you argue with them all the time. [Proverbs 18:19]

Reader: What do kind words and enjoying a good meal have in common?
Answer: They both have the ability to satisfy you. Food satisfies the stomach, words satisfy the heart.
[Proverbs 18:20]

Reader: How can I get my spouse to stay in love with me?
Answer: Be kind when you talk to them and don't raise your voice when you have a disagreement.

Your tongue has the power to kill your marriage or bring life to it. [Proverbs 18:21]

Reader: What blessing do you receive from God for marrying a godly wife?
Answer: His favor on your marriage. [Proverbs 18:22]

Reader: Why do some rich people take advantage of those who are poor?
Answer: They think that God is not watching, but He is and will punish them for their actions. [Proverbs 18:23]

Reader: How can I know that I've got a true friend?
Answer: When trouble comes, a true friend will come to your rescue. Fake friends run. [Proverbs 18:24]

Proverbs 19

Reader: What is a sign that a person lacks integrity?
Answer: They withhold information from people and don't tell them the truth. [Proverbs 19:1]

Reader: What is a sign that a person has integrity?
Answer: They admit when they've made a mistake instead of trying to hide it. [Proverbs 19:1]

Reader: How can I avoid making decisions based off my emotions?
Answer: Don't be in a hurry to say yes to every opportunity that comes your way. When someone presents you with an opportunity take a few days to think about it. You need to write down the pros and cons, get advice from friends and family members, and ask to God to help you make the right decision. [Proverbs 19:2]

Reader: Why is it that people blame God for all their problems?
Answer: They are ashamed to admit it was their fault. [Proverbs 19:3]

Reader: What do rich people have to be careful of?

Answer: Selecting their friends. When you're rich everyone wants to be your friend. [Proverbs 19:4]

Reader: Where are people most vulnerable to tell lies?
Answer: In court. [Proverbs 19:5]

Reader: What do some people do to get in good with people who are in high positions?
Answer: They flatter them and tell them how great and wonderful they are. They also give them gifts. [Proverbs 19:6]

Reader: If I have a relative that is poor should I avoid them?
Answer: No, always be willing to lend a helping hand when they need you. You might be the only family member they have to depend on. [Proverbs 19:7]

Reader: What do people do on a daily basis that love themselves?
Answer: They read God's Word. Reading the Bible is like working out in a gym. When you go to the gym to work out you work on your physical

appearance. When you read the Bible you work on your spiritual appearance. [Proverbs 19:8]

Reader: What does God think about people who lie in court just so their friend can go free?
Answer: He hates it. God will see to it that justice is served. [Proverbs 19:9]

Reader: How do fools become wealthy?
Answer: They either inherit money from their parents or they cheat people out of money. [Proverbs 19:10]

Reader: What is a way I can earn someone's respect?
Answer: Forgiving a person that's done you wrong. If you're willing to forgive them and not hold a grudge they'll appreciate you for having mercy on them. [Proverbs 19:11]

Reader: What is the difference between a good leader and a terrible one?
Answer: A good leader never takes out their frustrations on their employees if they're having a bad day. [Proverbs 19:12]

Reader: What does a high maintenance wife, and a rebellious child have in common?

Answer: They both get on your nerves. Your wife will complain that you don't do enough for her and your child will complain that you're always trying to tell them how to live their life. [Proverbs 19:13]

Reader: Is there anything that my biological father can't do for me?

Answer: Your biological father can give you material things like money, cars, and houses, but only God can give you a wise and understanding wife that loves you. [Proverbs 19:14]

Reader: What do lazy people do with most of their time?

Answer: They sleep it away, but they don't realize that the more you sleep, the less time you have to work and earn a living for yourself. [Proverbs 19:15]

Reader: Why does God want me to obey the Bible?

Answer: So you can live longer. Sin cuts your life short. [Proverbs 19:16]

Reader: When I help out poor people does God notice it?

Answer: Yes, He does. He will repay you for your kindness, He won't forget it. [Proverbs 19:17]

Reader: How can a parent ruin their child's life?

Answer: By not punishing them when they are young. Children need to learn discipline and respect at an early age because if they don't they will grow up and disrespect you and God. [Proverbs 19:18]

Reader: If my child has a hot temper, how can I put a stop to it?

Answer: Discipline them immediately. If you don't they'll think it's okay to misbehave. [Proverbs 19:19]

Reader: What are some things I can do to grow in wisdom?

Answer: Read and study the Bible consistently, and hang out with people who are wiser than you. [Proverbs 19:20]

Reader: Sometimes my plans don't turn out the way I want, is it my fault?

Answer: Sometimes God will alter your plans because He has a better one. [Proverbs 19:21]

Reader: What is the most attractive thing about a godly woman?
Answer: Her loyalty. When looking for a wife the first question you need to ask yourself is will she be loyal to you. If you don't feel in your heart that you can trust her then you shouldn't marry her. [Proverbs 19:22]

Reader: How can I safe guard myself from the Devil's traps?
Answer: Respect and obey God. When you're in God's will He can protect you from Satan, but when you rebel against God, you put your life in danger. [Proverbs 19:23]

Reader: What's a sign that a person is lazy?
Answer: They'd rather eat out or have others cook for them instead of feeding themselves. [Proverbs 19:24]

Reader: What do wise people do when they make mistakes?

Answer: They ask for advice so they won't make the same mistake twice. [Proverbs 19:25]

Reader: What do foolish people do when they make mistakes?
Answer: They continue making the same mistakes, because they're too prideful to ask for advice. [Proverbs 19:25]

Reader: When my parents get old and can't take care of themselves what should I do?
Answer: Be around them as much as possible, because when they're gone you won't be able to see them until you get to heaven. [Proverbs 19:26]

Reader: What's wrong with not going to church?
Answer: God wants you to learn about Him, what better place to learn about God than in church. [Proverbs 19:27]

Reader: What do evil people have in common with Satan?
Answer: They love to lie and hate justice and truth. [Proverbs 19:28]

Reader: What is the difference between a wise child and a foolish child?

Answer: Wise children obey their parents when they tell them to do something. Foolish children have to be disciplined before they will do what their parents say. [Proverbs 19:29]

Proverbs 20

Reader: What can make a person go from being calm and peaceful to mean and rowdy?
Answer: Alcohol. When a person drinks alcohol their personality changes and they become a different person. [Proverbs 20:1]

Reader: What is the easiest way to destroy your career?
Answer: Intentionally upsetting your supervisor. [Proverbs 20:2]

Reader: Why do couples breakup?
Answer: Because they argue and fight all the time. They can't control their emotions so they take out their frustrations on each other instead of loving each other. [Proverbs 20:3]

Reader: How do people miss out on promotions?
Answer: They're not prepared and lack work ethic. [Proverbs 20:4]

Reader: How can I get my wife to open up to me?

Answer: Be a good listener. The more you listen, the more she will want to share with you her deepest thoughts and feelings. [Proverbs 20:5]

Reader: What quality do all women want their husbands to have?
Answer: Loyalty. When a man is loyal to his wife, her self-esteem is higher and she's happier. [Proverbs 20:6]

Reader: Can the way I live affect my kids?
Answer: Children model what they see. If you set a godly example for them, then when they're older they'll be godly as well. [Proverbs 20:7]

Reader: What does a good leader do when faced with a decision?
Answer: They weigh all their options. They never make a decision before they've thought through every option first. [Proverbs 20:8]

Reader: What is something that I'll never be?
Answer: Perfect. You're going to miss the mark and sin. When you do fall short ask God for forgiveness. [Proverbs 20:9]

Reader: How does God want me to conduct business deals?
Answer: He wants them to be fair and reasonable. God hates it when people are cheated out of their money. [Proverbs 20:10]

Reader: Can children be wiser than adults?
Answer: A child that is wise at an early age will be wiser than an adult that is a fool. [Proverbs 20:11]

Reader: What two gifts does God give babies when they're born?
Answer: Ears to hear and eyes to see. [Proverbs 20:12]

Reader: What can I do to master my craft?
Answer: Sleep less and work more. The more you sleep the less time you'll have to perfect your craft. [Proverbs 20:13]

Reader: What should I be careful of when negotiating with a car salesman?
Answer: They might try to sell you a car that's not worth the retail price. Make sure you do your homework on how much the car is really worth. [Proverbs 20:14]

Reader: What's rarer than gold and rubies?
Answer: People who speak with wisdom. The world is filled with people who speak mean and vicious words, but it's rare when you find someone that speaks with wisdom and intelligence. [Proverbs 20:15]

Reader: Should I invest money into a person who is struggling financially?
Answer: Be very cautious. They might take your money and use it for another business deal that you have no clue about and you'll never see your money again. [Proverbs 20:16]

Reader: Why do people steal?
Answer: Because it's an adrenaline rush, but they don't realize that after their high dies down, they're one step closer to going to jail for the crime they committed. [Proverbs 20:17]

Reader: Why is it important I get advice from a trusted friend before making a critical decision?
Answer: They can point out dangers and risks that you haven't thought about and don't see. [Proverbs 20:18]

Reader: Why should I stay away from people who gossip?
Answer: If you tell a gossiper confidential information they will tell others what the two of you discussed. [Proverbs 20:19]

Reader: When a child grows up and leaves home, what should they give their parents?
Answer: Respect. Just because you don't live at home anymore doesn't mean that you don't have to respect your parents anymore. [Proverbs 20:20]

Reader: Should parents give their children lump sums of money at an early age?
Answer: No, because they may not use it wisely. [Proverbs 20:21]

Reader: Someone I know stole from me.
Answer: Don't seek revenge. Let God handle the matter. He knows just what to do to pay them back for what they did to you. [Proverbs 20:22]

Reader: Why is God offended when people cheat others out of money?

Answer: When a person works hard for their money and someone comes along and cheats them out of it, it angers God. [Proverbs 20:23]

Reader: What can I do to relieve stress in my life?
Answer: Quit trying to figure out what God is going to do in your future and focus on today. [Proverbs 20:24]

Reader: Why shouldn't I make a promise to God?
Answer: Because you may not be able to keep it. God doesn't require that you make promises to Him because it places added pressure on you to obey Him. [Proverbs 20:25]

Reader: If an associate is stealing money from the company they work for, what should the manager do?
Answer: Fire the associate immediately. The longer they stay employed the more money they'll take out of your pocket and your employee's pockets. [Proverbs 20:26]

Reader: Is it possible to read someone's thoughts?

Answer: The only person that can read your thoughts is God. He knows about everything you think about. [Proverbs 20:27]

Reader: How do employees feel about a boss that treats them fairly?
Answer: They love them and will go to bat for them. [Proverbs 20:28]

Reader: What is the best thing about being young?
Answer: You have energy and strength. [Proverbs 20:29]

Reader: What is the best thing about being old?
Answer: Having gray hair from living a life that pleased God. [Proverbs 20:29]

Reader: How does God get a person's attention so that they turn back to Him?
Answer: He lets life beat them up. [Proverbs 20:30]

Proverbs 21

Reader: How can a person go from being a good leader to a great leader?
Answer: By letting God direct their decisions. Leaders make lots of important decisions throughout the day. If they want to ensure that they're making the best decisions possible they need to look at situations from God's perspective. [Proverbs 21:1]

Reader: What can stop me from making a decision that I'll later regret?
Answer: Don't make decisions with the wrong motives. Being honest with yourself will help you make better decisions. [Proverbs 21:2]

Reader: What is religious performance?
Answer: It's when you strive to earn blessings from God. When you focus more on the blessings than on God, then you miss out on the blessings. God doesn't bless religious performance; because He knows that once you get what you desire you won't obey Him anymore. [Proverbs 21:3]

Reader: How can I overcome religious performance?
Answer: When you obey God do it because you want Him to be happy, then the blessings will come. Every sin and temptation is an attempt to stop you from bringing happiness to God. Disobedience breaks God's heart, obedience gets God excited! [Proverbs 21:3]

Reader: What's a sign that a person is arrogant?
Answer: They don't like to congratulate you when you achieve success. [Proverbs 20:4]

Reader: How can I become successful at my craft?
Answer: Dedicate your time and energy to it. You might have to wake up early and go to bed late, but it'll be well worth it. There are no shortcuts to success. Proverbs 20:5]

Reader: Why do some people go bankrupt over night?
Answer: Because they lied and cheated to gain their wealth. [Proverbs 21:6]

Reader: Why is there so much violence in the world?

Answer: Because people are not willing to work to earn a living. They would rather rob someone of their wealth than get a job. [Proverbs 21:7]

Reader: What does guilt cause a person to do?
Answer: Hide, cheat, and steal to cover up their wrong doing. [Proverbs 21:8]

Reader: What does integrity cause you to do?
Answer: It causes a person to be honest, fair, and have peace because they don't have anything to cover up. [Proverbs 21:8]

Reader: Does it do you any good to marry a woman that's beautiful, but complains a lot?
Answer: No. You won't notice her beauty if she's constantly getting on your nerves with her nagging. [Proverbs 21:9]

Reader: Should I let a friend live with me that is always in trouble.
Answer: No, if you do you won't have any peace. [Proverbs 21:10]

Reader: Can a wise person learn from a fool?

Answer: When a wise person sees a fool get punished for being disobedient, the wise person will take notice so they won't make the same mistake. [Proverbs 21:11]

Reader: I have a secret that my spouse doesn't know about.
Answer: It's best that you tell them, if you don't God will expose you. [Proverbs 21:12]

Reader: Why should I help people who are in need?
Answer: Because you never know when you might need a favor yourself. [Proverbs 21:13]

Reader: How can you calm down a person who's really angry?
Answer: Give them a gift. [Proverbs 21:14]

Reader: Why do evil people hate justice?
Answer: They are afraid of going to prison for the crimes they've committed. [Proverbs 21:15]

Reader: Why do some people die before their time?
Answer: They put themselves in dangerous situations. [Proverbs 21:16]

Reader: How can I gain financial freedom?
Answer: Don't spend your money on things you don't need. [Proverbs 21:17]

Reader: Why does God punish wicked people?
Answer: To protect His children from being harmed by them. [Proverbs 21:18]

Reader: What happens when a husband refuses to love and cherish his wife?
Answer: She loses respect for him and talks down to him. [Proverbs 21:19]

Reader: If I get a raise at work, what should I do with the money?
Answer: Save it and put it in the bank. [Proverbs 21:20]

Reader: What is the payoff for trying to live a godly life?
Answer: You will receive love and honor from God. [Proverbs 21:21]

Reader: What is the best way to overcome a sin I'm struggling with?

Answer: Read the Bible and find out what God says about the particular sin and do what He says. [Proverbs 21:22]

Reader: Should I tell everyone about my future goals and plans?
Answer: Tell only the people that have your best interest at heart. If you tell the wrong people they might try to ruin your dream. [Proverbs 21:23]

Reader: What does an arrogant person do when they achieve success?
Answer: They take the credit instead of giving it to God. [Proverbs 21:24]

Reader: What do lazy people think about?
Answer: How successful they're going to be, but they refuse to work to make their dreams become reality. [Proverbs 21:25]

Reader: What ruins marriages?
Answer: Stinginess. Marriage is all about sharing. If you're not willing to share your money and time with your spouse your marriage will fall apart. If you want to have a successful marriage be a giver not a taker. [Proverbs 21:26]

Reader: What does God hate about evil people?
Answer: When they try to act godly just to get
something from Him in their time of need.
[Proverbs 21:27]

Reader: When a witness testifies falsely on the
stand, what does the lawyer need to do?
Answer: Put a credible witness on the stand to tell
the truth so that the person who lied under oath
will be exposed. [Proverbs 21:28]

Reader: What should I do if I'm asked to do
something I don't know how to do?
Answer: Be honest and tell the person you don't
know how to do it. They will appreciate the fact
that you were honest with them and told them the
truth. [Proverbs 21:29]

Reader: Why do people think they can get
something over on God?
Answer: Because they think He's not watching
what they're doing, but in reality, God's paying
close attention. [Proverbs 21:30]

Reader: What should I remember when I become successful?
Answer: That your abilities came from God. Always give God credit for your success. [Proverbs 21:31]

Proverbs 22

Reader: What's better than having a large amount of money in your bank account?
Answer: Having an exceptional reputation. [Proverbs 22:1]

Reader: Do rich people and poor people have anything in common?
Answer: They both were made by God. [Proverbs 22:2]

Reader: If I work with a woman that's attractive how can I avoid cheating on my wife?
Answer: Take precautions not to spend lengthy periods of time with her. The more you admire her beauty, the more you'll have thoughts of sleeping with her. [Proverbs 22:3]

Reader: Some people say that being humble and respecting God will get you nowhere in life.
Answer: They're wrong. Respecting God and being humble will lead to riches, honor, and a long life. [Proverbs 22:4]

Reader: What do police officers need to watch out for?
Answer: Criminals will try to offer police officers bribes so they won't have to go to jail. [Proverbs 22:5]

Reader: What is music to a parent's ears?
Answer: Hearing their children tell them thank you for raising them the right way. [Proverbs 22:6]

Reader: What should I consider before buying an item?
Answer: If you can afford it. Try not to pay credit for the item if you know you're going to have a hard time paying the money back. [Proverbs 22:7]

Reader: How should I handle someone trying to intimidate me?
Answer: Don't seek revenge. God will punish them for trying to intimidate you. [Proverbs 22:8]

Reader: Volunteering at a soup kitchen doesn't earn you any money.
Answer: Yes, it does. Feeding the poor is like you feeding God; He'll reward you for your service and sacrifice. [Proverbs 22:9]

Reader: What's the best way to rid your company of arguing and fighting amongst co-workers?
Answer: Fire the person who's purposely causing division within your company. [Proverbs 22:10]

Reader: What do managers like their associates to exhibit at work?
Answer: Strong character and wise speech. No manager wants to hire an employee that has weak character and a nasty mouth. [Proverbs 22:11]

Reader: What is beautiful about knowledge?
Answer: It can save your life. [Proverbs 22:12]

Reader: What do lazy people do to avoid work?
Answer: They make excuses. [Proverbs 22:13]

Reader: I'm a single man. Is there anything wrong with a married woman frequently complimenting me?
Answer: Be cautious. She might be trying to seduce you into sleeping with her by stroking your ego with her compliments. Stay away from her. [Proverbs 22:14]

Reader: My child likes to talk back to me, what can I do to fix this?
Answer: Discipline them until they learn to show you the respect you deserve. [Proverbs 22:15]

Reader: If I spend all my money showering people with unnecessary gifts to impress them, what'll happen?
Answer: You will go bankrupt. [Proverbs 22:16]

Reader: What is the purpose of studying the thirty wise sayings?
Answer: So that you'll learn to trust God and be successful.

Reader: Should I memorize theses sayings?
Answer: Yes, you never know when you might need to use them. [Proverbs 22:17-21]

1. Don't cheat people out of money and turn around and take them to court. They will lose the case because they can't afford a lawyer to prove their innocence. [Proverbs 22:22-23]

2. Don't hang out with people with quick tempers, because they will rub off on you. [Proverbs 22:24-25]

3. Don't co-sign a loan because you take the chance of ruining your credit. [Proverbs 22:26-27]

4. Don't cheat people out of their land and sell it for profit. [Proverbs 22:28]

5. Perfect your gifts and talents. When you're excellent at what you do, you'll get noticed by powerful individuals. [Proverbs 22:29]

Proverbs 23

6. When invited out to dinner with someone influential eat light. If you eat too much they will think you're greedy. [Proverbs 23:1-3]

7. Instead of focusing all your attention on building up your bank account, focus on building up your character. Money comes and goes, but your character is priceless. [Proverbs 23:4-5]

8. Stay away from greedy people, they smile in your face and talk behind your back. [Proverbs 23:6-8]

9. Don't give advice to people who think they know everything, they won't listen to you. [Proverbs 23:9]

10. Don't cheat people out of their land just because you want it. [Proverbs 23:10-11]

11. Pay attention to people who are wise. You can learn a thing or two from them. [Proverbs 23:12]

12. When your children misbehave punish them. [Proverbs 23:13-14]

13. Read and study the Bible consistently. [Proverbs 23:15-16]

14. Don't be jealous of sinful people's success. [Proverbs 23:17-18]

15. Don't hang out with people who like to get drunk. [Proverbs 23:19-21]

16. Always respect your parents. [Proverbs 23:22-25]

17. Only have sex with your spouse. [Proverbs 23:26-28]

18. Don't get addicted to alcohol and drugs. [Proverbs 23:29-35]

Proverbs 24

19. Don't hang out with people who are criminals and corrupt. [Proverbs 24:1-2]

20. Before buying a home make sure you can afford it. [Proverbs 24:3-4]

21. Your success depends on who you get advice from. [Proverbs 24:5-6]

22. Don't discuss important matters with foolish people. [Proverbs 24:7]

23. Don't be a troublemaker. [Proverbs 24:8-9]

24. If your character is weak, then you won't be able to handle adversity. [Proverbs 24:10]

25. If people are in trouble and you have the power to help them do it. [Proverbs 24:11-12]

26. If you love the Bible, you will be successful at whatever you do. [Proverbs 24:13-14]

27. Don't mistreat godly people. [Proverbs 24:15-16]

28. Don't celebrate if your enemy gets in trouble. [Proverbs 24:17-18]

29. Don't worry about corrupt individuals who are successful. [Proverbs 24:19-20]

30. Respect God and people in authority. [Proverbs 24:21-22]

Reader: Is it wrong to show favoritism in the court of law?
Answer: Yes, the judge who lets innocent people go to prison and sets the guilty free will be cursed. Judges that convict the guilty will be blessed. [Proverbs 24:23-25]

Reader: Sometimes I hate hearing the truth.
Answer: Hearing the truth is better than hearing a lie. A true friend will tell you what you don't want to hear. [Proverbs 24:26]

Reader: Before I get married, what do I need to do?

Answer: Learn how to budget the money you make. [Proverbs 24:27]

Reader: Is getting along with your neighbors important?
Answer: Yes, don't lie on your neighbors and make accusations against them that aren't true. [Proverbs 24:28-29]

Reader: Is it possible for a person to rob themselves?
Answer: Yes, by sleeping too much. Sleeping too much robs you of the time you need to work toward your future goals. [Proverbs 24:30-34]

Proverbs 25

Reader: Did anyone help contribute to the Book of Proverbs besides Solomon?
Answer: King Hezekiah had a group of scribes contribute to the Book of Proverbs. [Proverbs 25:1]

Reader: Does God have any secrets?
Answer: Once you dig into God's Word and get to know Him, He will reveal to you secrets on how to be successful in the areas you struggle in. [Proverbs 25:2]

Reader: Should a leader reveal everything to the people they're over?
Answer: No, certain information needs to be kept confidential. [Proverbs 25:3]

Reader: How can managers hurt their company?
Answer: By placing people in roles of authority that lack integrity and aren't reliable. [Proverbs 25:4-5]

Reader: What should I not do to people in authority?

Answer: Don't brag on yourself and your accomplishments. Only talk about yourself if you're asked to. [Proverbs 25:6-7]

Reader: Should I make an accusation without having proof the person did it?
Answer: When you have a dispute, don't accuse the person of wrong doing until you have concrete proof. If you accuse someone of doing something wrong and they are innocent, you will damage your reputation. [Proverbs 25:7-8]

Reader: What can happen if I tell another person's secret that they told me not to tell anyone else?
Answer: You'll be known as a gossiper and the person's secret you told will hate you. Anytime someone tells you something confidential keep their information private. [Proverbs 25:9-10]

Reader: If someone asks me for advice, what is the one thing I need to remember?
Answer: Give them the advice they need in a timely manner. Don't make them wait forever. [Proverbs 25:11]

Reader: Should I listen to criticism?

Answer: Yes, especially if it's valid and comes from a person who loves you and wants the best for you. [Proverbs 25:12]

Reader: What can I do to impress my boss?
Answer: Be trustworthy. [Proverbs 25:13]

Reader: If I promise my wife I'm going to do something and I don't do it, how will she feel?
Answer: She will resent you and lose respect for you. It's better just to say I can't do it than to make a promise and break your word. [Proverbs 25:14]

Reader: How can being patient benefit me?
Answer: Powerful people will want you to work for them because they know you won't walk out and quit when things get rough. [Proverbs 25:15]

Reader: How can I get my point across to someone I'm mad at?
Answer: Use a soft tone of voice. Tell the person how you feel without raising your voice and yelling at them. [Proverbs 25:15]

Reader: Is it possible to become addicted to things other than gambling, sex, drugs, and alcohol?

Answer: Anything can become addictive if you do it too much. [Proverbs 25:16]

Reader: Should I visit my friends all the time?
Answer: No, if you do they will get tired of you. [Proverbs 25:17]

Reader: Why is telling lies about people so dangerous?
Answer: One lie or false accusation can damage a person's reputation forever. [Proverbs 25:18]

Reader: What's something that every wife needs from her husband?
Answer: For him to be there in times of trouble and not run when things get rough. [Proverbs 25:19]

Reader: When a person is going through a hard time what should I not do?
Answer: Don't tell them jokes and laugh about the situation. Comfort and console them. [Proverbs 25:20]

Reader: If my enemy is in trouble, what should I do?

Answer: Offer to help them. By doing this they will be ashamed of themselves and God will reward you. [Proverbs 25:21-22]

Reader: What does gossip cause?
Answer: Anger. When people are angry they become outraged and want revenge for what was said about them. [Proverbs 25:23]

Reader: What can ruin a beautiful home?
Answer: A nagging and complaining wife. [Proverbs 25:24]

Reader: What can turn around a person's day if they're going through a lot?
Answer: Giving them good news about how to overcome the trial they are facing. [Proverbs: 25:25]

Reader: Should I compromise my sexual standards just to please another person.
Answer: No, if they don't respect your standards then don't date them. [Proverbs 25:26]

Reader: What can make a person sick to their stomach?

Answer: A person that always bragging on themselves. [Proverbs 25:27]

Reader: Why is self-control so important?
Answer: Without self-control, you will be controlled by your emotions and you will do things that you know aren't good for you. [Proverbs 25:28]

Proverbs 26

Reader: How should I handle foolish people?
Answer: There are ten things you need to
remember when dealing with foolish people:

1. Don't give them positions of power.
    [Proverbs 26:1]
2. If they wish you bad luck, it will come to
    them instead of you. [Proverbs 26:2]
3. They hate to be corrected, they won't learn
    until their life is in jeopardy. [Proverbs 26:3]
4. They like to argue about things that don't
    matter. [Proverbs 26:4]
5. If they try to debate you about the Bible
    answer their questions respectfully.
    [Proverbs 26:5]
6. They can't be trusted so don't tell them
    confidential information. [Proverbs 26:6]
7. They know what the Bible says, but refuse
    to believe it. [Proverbs 26:7]
8. Don't honor and praise them. [Proverbs
    26:8]
9. Don't seek advice from them. [Proverbs
    26:9]
10. Don't hire them to work for you. [Proverbs
    26:10]

Reader: Is it a good idea to date someone you've dated several times already?
Answer: No. The same thing they did to cause the break up they'll do again. [Proverbs 26:11]

Reader: Why is it hard for some people to realize they've made a mistake?
Answer: Pride. Thinking you're right all the time will prevent you from seeing your shortcomings. [Proverbs 26:12]

Reader: What do lazy people do that prevent them from being successful?
Answer: Lazy people do four things:
1. They make up excuses to get out of working. [Proverbs 26:13]
2. They sleep all the time. [Proverbs 26:14]
3. They want other people to feed them. [Proverbs 26:15]
4. They think they know everything. [Proverbs 26:16]

Reader: If I see two people arguing should I get involved?

Answer: Never interfere in matters that don't concern you. If they don't ask you for your opinion, mind your own business. [Proverbs 26:17]

Reader: What do gossipers do when they get caught in a lie?
Answer: They say they were only joking. [Proverbs 26:18-19]

Reader: How do arguments get started amongst people in work and school?
Answer: Gossip. When gossip is passed from one person to another it spreads like a deadly virus. [Proverbs 26:20]

Reader: What about people who start arguments?
Answer: Arguments kill relationships just like diseases kill people. [Proverbs 26:21]

Reader: Why are rumors dangerous?
Answer: They are hard to forget. The person who the rumor is about will have a hard time blocking it out their mind. [Proverbs 26:22]

Reader: How can I know if someone is my enemy?

Answer: If they are bold enough to tell you they hate another person to your face, then they will say the same thing about you behind your back. [Proverbs 26:23]

Reader: Can flattery harm you?
Answer: When someone is constantly being flattered their guard goes down. When your guard is down you become vulnerable. [Proverbs 26:24-26]

Reader: What should I never do to another person?
Answer: Set a trap for them to get revenge for something they did to you. If you set a trap for someone else, you will fall into it yourself. [Proverbs 26:27]

Reader: What can cause a person to cheat on their spouse?
Answer: Listening to the compliments of a person that's not your spouse. [Proverbs 26:28]

Proverbs 27

Reader: What do fools brag about?
Answer: What they're going to do in the future. Wise people keep their mouths shut and put in work. [Proverbs 27:1]

Reader: Should I brag on myself?
Answer: Let others brag on you. When you brag on yourself you'll get a reputation as being arrogant. [Proverbs 27:2]

Reader: What can weigh a person down?
Answer: Having to be around foolish people all the time. [Proverbs 27:3]

Reader: What can destroy a relationship?
Answer: Jealousy. When you're dating someone that's jealous they want to control you and know your every move. [Proverbs 27:4]

Reader: If I have a problem with my spouse how should I handle it?
Answer: Tell them the truth in love. Your spouse can't fix the problem unless they know about it. It

might hurt, but they'll appreciate your honesty. [Proverbs 27:5-6]

Reader: What should I do with leftover food?
Answer: Give it to someone who needs it. Just because you don't want it doesn't mean somebody else won't enjoy it. [Proverbs 27:7]

Reader: What should married couples never do?
Answer: Spend enormous amounts of time away from home. If you spend most of your time hanging out with your friends visiting them instead of being home with your spouse your marriage will suffer. [Proverbs 27:8]

Reader: How can I know I've got a real friend?
Answer: They tell you what you need to hear instead of what you want to hear. [Proverbs 27:9]

Reader: Why is it good to have at least one or two friends you can count on?
Answer: When you need help you will have someone to be there for you. [Proverbs 27:10]

Reader: Why is it important that I learn the Bible?

Answer: When people criticize your faith you'll be able to defend it. [Proverbs 27:11]

Reader: What can I do to prevent myself from making a bad decision that I might regret?
Answer: Think about the consequences. [Proverbs 27:12]

Reader: How can I know if someone doesn't have financial integrity?
Answer: They expect something for nothing. [Proverbs 27:13]

Reader: I'm an early riser and my spouse is a night owl. Is this a problem?
Answer: The only way it will be a problem is if you wake up making a lot of noise. Try to wake up as quietly as possible, that way your spouse can get the rest they need without being disturbed. [Proverbs 27:14]

Reader: What can ruin a marriage?
Answer: A wife that complains all the time. Instead of complaining to your husband, complement him instead. [Proverbs 27:15-16]

Reader: What's the difference between an acquaintance and a friend?
Answer: An acquaintance will listen to your goals; a friend will help you achieve them. [Proverbs 27:17]

Reader: If I have a good employee that works hard, how can I reward them?
Answer: Increase their pay or promote them to a higher position. [Proverbs 27:18]

Reader: How can I know what is going in a person's mind?
Answer: Listen to their words and look at their facial expressions. [Proverbs 27:19]

Reader: I have a void in my life. I've tried to fill it with relationships and material things. What should I do?
Answer: Whatever you enjoy that God has gifted you to do, do that to fill the void. [Proverbs 27:20]

Reader: What is an effective way to see if a person is stuck up?
Answer: Give them a compliment a see how they respond to it. [Proverbs 27:21]

Reader: Why do certain people refuse to change?
Answer: They don't feel they have to, even though their life is a mess. [Proverbs 27:22]

Reader: How can I ensure that I'll have money to live off of in the future?
Answer: Work hard now while you have the strength, invest your money wisely, and don't spend it all. [Proverbs 27:23-27]

Proverbs 28

Reader: What are some signs that a person is a bad leader?
Answer:

1. They're sneaky. [Proverbs 28:1]
2. They rebel against authority. [Proverbs 28:2]
3. They oppress the poor. [Proverbs 28:3]
4. They reject the Word of God. [Proverbs 28:4]
5. They hate justice. [Proverbs 28:5]
6. They're dishonest. [Proverbs 28:6]
7. They hang out with people who love to sin. [Proverbs 28:7]
8. They cheat people out of money. [Proverbs 28:8]
9. Their prayers don't get heard by God. [Proverbs 28:9]
10. They trick people to get what they want. [Proverbs 28:10]
11. They think they're smarter than you. [Proverbs 28:11]
12. They make life miserable for the people they supervise. [Proverbs 28:12]
13. The hide their sins. [Proverbs 28:13]

14. They're stubborn. [Proverbs 28:14]
15. They intimidate people that make less money than they do. [Proverbs 28:15]
16. They try to bully you. [Proverbs 28:16]
17. They try to murder people's character. [Proverbs 28:17]
18. They tell lies and expect to get away with it. [Proverbs 28:18]
19. They'd rather chase a fantasy than roll up their sleeves and go to work. [Proverbs 28:19]
20. They take their money and invest it in get-rich quick schemes. [Proverbs 28:20]
21. They show favoritism to people they like. [Proverbs 28:21]
22. They're selfish. [Proverbs 28:22]
23. They'd rather you flatter them than tell them the truth. [Proverbs 28:23]
24. They steal from their family. [Proverbs 28:24]
25. They trust themselves more than they trust God. [Proverbs 28:25]
26. They hate when people give them advice. [Proverbs 28:26]
27. They're stingy with their money. [Proverbs 28:27]

28. They're corrupt. [Proverbs 28:28]

Proverbs 29

Reader: How can I tell if someone is a great leader?
Answer:

1. They accept valid criticism. [Proverbs 29:1]
2. When they get promoted people celebrate. [Proverbs 29:2]
3. They're faithful to their spouse. [Proverbs 29:3]
4. They bring stability to their country. [Proverbs 29:4]
5. They tell their friends the truth in love. [Proverbs 29:5]
6. They don't get themselves entangled in addictions. [Proverbs 29:6]
7. They care about the rights of the poor. [Proverbs 29:7]
8. They know how to calm people down. [Proverbs 29:8]
9. They hire wise lawyers to defend them in court. [Proverbs 29:9]
10. They love to help the poor. [Proverbs 29:10]
11. When they're angry they hold it in until they cool off. [Proverbs 29:11]
12. They don't pay attention to liars. [Proverbs 29:12]

13. They recognize their physical health is a gift from God. [Proverbs 29:13]
14. They're compassionate to those whose income is less than their own. [Proverbs 29:14]
15. They discipline their children. [Proverbs 29:15]
16. Sin reduces when they're in charge. [Proverbs 29:16]
17. Their children reflect themselves. [Proverbs 29:17]
18. They obey the Bible. [Proverbs 29:18]
19. When someone gives them good advice they take it. [Proverbs 29:19]
20. They think before they speak. [Proverbs 29:20]
21. They don't spoil their children. [Proverbs 29:21]
22. They control their emotions. [Proverbs 29:22]
23. They're humble. [Proverbs 29:23]
24. They don't steal money. [Proverbs 29:24]
25. They trust God more than they trust anyone else, including themselves. [Proverbs 29:25]
26. They rely on God to help them lead the people they're over. [Proverbs 29:26]

27. They despise people who intentionally hurt others. [Proverbs 29:27]

Proverbs 30

Reader: What will reading the Bible make me realize about myself?
Answer: That you're not as smart and intelligent as you think you are. [Proverbs 30:1-3]

Reader: How does God display his power to us?
Answer: Look outside at the sky. Look at the sun, moon, and stars. God created it. [Proverbs 30:4-5]

Reader: What is something God has never done?
Answer: Told a lie. [Proverbs 30:5]

Reader: When it comes to God protecting me from danger, what do I need to remember?
Answer: The only way God can protect you is if you do what He says. [Proverbs 30:5]

Reader: What should I never do to the Bible?
Answer: Say things that's not in it. [Proverbs 30:6]

Reader: Is there anything specifically that God wants me to pray for?
Answer: He wants you to pray for integrity and contentment. If you have integrity you won't cheat

people out money and cheat on your spouse. If you're content with what you have and cherish it, God can bless you with more. [Proverbs 30:7-9]

Reader: If I have a disagreement with a co-worker, what should I never do?
Answer: Handle the matter privately. Don't slander the associate to your co-workers. [Proverbs 30:10]

Reader: What should I do on Mother's Day and Father's Day?
Answer: Thank your parents for all they've done for you. [Proverbs 30:11]

Reader: What if I don't have a good relationship with my parents?
Answer: Call them anyway. God will reward you for doing it. [Proverbs 30:11]

Reader: What should I never tell myself?
Answer: That you're perfect. [Proverbs 30:12]

Reader: How do corrupt people make their living?
Answer: They take advantage of the poor. [Proverbs 30:13-14]

Reader: How can I know if a person is selfish?
Answer: No matter what you do for them they're never satisfied, they always want more. [Proverbs 30:15]

Reader: How can I know if someone is greedy?
Answer: There are four ways to know if a person is greedy.
1. They take more than they give.
2. They're jealous of people who have what they don't have.
3. They never say thank you.
4. They cheat to get ahead. [Proverbs 30:16]

Reader: What happens to children who disrespect their parents?
Answer: God will judge them for it. [Proverbs 30:17]

Reader: What is more amazing than an eagle flying in the sky, a snake crawling on the ground, and a ship sailing on the sea?
Answer: The passion between a husband and wife. [Proverbs 30:18-19]

Reader: What is the number one excuse married couples give for cheating on their spouse?
Answer: My needs weren't getting met. [Proverbs 30:20]

Reader: What can make my life miserable?
Answer: Four things can make your life miserable.
1. Having authority and power that you don't know how to use.
2. Having no one in your life to give you honest advice.
3. Marrying the wrong spouse.
4. Having an affair. [Proverbs 30:21-23]

Reader: Can animals teach us about life?
Answer: Yes, several animals can teach us about life. [Proverbs 30:24]
1. Ants teach you how to be disciplined. [Proverbs 30:25]
2. Rock badgers teach you how to be cautious and avoid danger. [Proverbs 30:26]
3. Locusts teach you how to work with others. [Proverbs 30:27]
4. Lizards teach you how not to panic. [Proverbs 30:28]

5. Lions teach you not to fear people.
   [Proverbs 30:29-30]
6. Roosters and goats teach you how to submit to God. [Proverbs 30:31]

Reader: What do kings and husbands have in common?
Answer: Kings lead their troops. Husbands lead their families. [Proverbs 30:31]

Reader: What does pride cause you to do?
Answer: It makes you paranoid that someone else wants what you have. [Proverbs 30:32]

Reader: What can I expect if I get into an argument with someone?
Answer: For them to retaliate. [Proverbs 30:33]

Proverbs 31

Reader: What should parents teach their kids at an early age?
Answer: They should teach them the importance of waiting to marriage to have sex. [Proverbs 31:1-3]

Reader: What will happen if I get drunk off alcohol and high off drugs?
Answer: Drugs and alcohol alter your mind. When your senses are impaired and you can't think straight you make dumb decisions. [Proverbs 31:4-5]

Reader: Some people I know drink alcohol and get high to forget about their problems.
Answer: Alcohol and drugs can only bring temporary relief from hurt and pain. God is the only person that can help you cope with your problems. [Proverbs 31:5-7]

Reader: Who should I stand up for?
Answer: People that can't defend themselves. If you see someone that is being taking advantage of come to their rescue. [Proverbs 31:8-9]

Reader: What do women need to understand about themselves?

Answer: Their value. When you go to shopping stores they normally have a discount rack. A virtuous woman will never be on a clearance rack. Women should have the mentality that if you're not willing to pay full price for me then you can't have me. [Proverbs 31:10]

Reader: What do singles need to ask themselves about the person they are dating before marriage?

Answer: Can I trust them, and will they make me a better person. [Proverbs 31:11]

Reader: A lot of marriages fall apart after three or four years. Why is this?

Answer: They start taking each other for granted. [Proverbs 31:12]

Reader: What kind of characteristics does a godly wife have?

Answer: A godly wife:

1. Makes sure her family is well dressed. [Proverbs 31:13]
2. She makes sure her family is well fed. [Proverbs 31:14]

3. She wakes up early so she can prepare for her day. [Proverbs 31:15]
4. She spends her money wisely. [Proverbs 31:16]
5. She has a great work ethic. [Proverbs 31:17]
6. She stays up late to finish her task. [Proverbs 31:18]
7. She perfects her gift and talents. [Proverbs 31:19]
8. She helps people in need. [Proverbs 31:20]
9. She makes sure her family has warm clothes for the winter. [Proverbs 31:21]
10. She makes sure her bedroom is well decorated and clean. [Proverbs 31:22]
11. She takes care of her body and cares about her appearance. [Proverbs 31:22]
12. She enhances her husband's reputation because of her character. [Proverbs 31:23]
13. She uses her gifts and talents to create income for her family. [Proverbs 31:24]
14. She cares more about her inner beauty than her outer beauty. [Proverbs 31:25]
15. She's excited about her family's future. [Proverbs 31:25]
16. She uses her words wisely and stays away from gossip. [Proverbs 31:26]

17. She protects her husband and children from anyone or anything that might pose a threat to them. [Proverbs 31:27]

Reader: What can children do to let their mother know they appreciate her?
Answer: Tell her thank you for all that she's done for you and how special she is. [Proverbs 31:28]

Reader: What about her husband?
Answer: He should praise her as well. [Proverbs 31:29]

Reader: What should ever man think about his wife?
Answer: That he married the greatest woman in the world. Not only should he think this, but he should also show her. [Proverbs 31:29]

Reader: How much value should I place on looks when it comes to a spouse?
Answer: There's nothing wrong with wanting to marry an attractive spouse, just remember they won't look the same forever. A spouse that loves God is the most attractive attribute a person can have. [Proverbs 31:30]

Reader: Why is that?

Answer: The more your spouse loves God, the more they'll love you. [Proverbs 31:30]

Reader: How can I let my wife know how much she means to me?

Answer: Praise her in front of others, and praise her when the two of you are alone. She will be tickled pink! [Proverbs 31:31]

Index

Bible

- 2:1-6
- 4:20-22
- 6:20-24
- 10:14
- 13:6
- 15:23

Bragging

- 12:23

Career

- 11:2
- 11:10-11
- 12:14
- 12:24
- 13:14
- 14:4
- 14:7

Constructive criticism

- 15:31-32

Crime

- 4:14-17
- 6:12-14
- 6:15
- 10:10
- 11:16
- 12:17
- 14:5
- 14:25
- 14:33

Dating

- 4:18-19
- 11:3
- 11:22
- 12:4
- 13:20
- 14:15
- 15:28

- 15:30

Death

- 10:7
- 11:4
- 11:7
- 11:19
- 12:7
- 13:22

Decision making

- 13:16

Dishonesty

- 12:19
- 12:22
- 13:5
- 13:15

Fear of God

- 1:7

Fighting

- 3:29-30

Food

- 12:27

Forgiveness

- 14:9

Friendship

- 11:30
- 14:21

God

- 3:11-12
- 3:31-32
- 3:33
- 3:34
- 6:16-19
- 9:10
- 10:6
- 10:29
- 11:8
- 11:21
- 11:31
- 12:2
- 13:21
- 13:25
- 14:2
- 14:11
- 14:22
- 14:26
- 14:27
- 14:31
- 14:32
- 15:3
- 15:9
- 15:10
- 15:11
- 15:26
- 15:33

Health

- 3:1
- 3:2
- 4:10
- 4:23
- 10:27
- 14:30

Heaven/Hell

- 12:28
- 15:24

Integrity

- 2:9-11
- 10:9
- 11:5

- 11:20

Intelligence

- 12:8
- 15:14

Laziness

- 10:26
- 13:4
- 15:19

Marriage

- 2:16-19
- 2:20-22
- 11:29
- 12:11
- 12:15
- 12:25
- 14:1
- 14:12
- 15:6

- 15:17
- 15:18
- 15:25
- 15:27

Money

- 1:19
- 3:3-4
- 3:9-10
- 3:14-18
- 6:1-5
- 10:2
- 10:4
- 10:12
- 10:15
- 10:16
- 10:22
- 11:1
- 11:15
- 11:18
- 11:24-25
- 11:26
- 11:28
- 12:12

- 13:7
- 13:8
- 13:11
- 13:23
- 14:20
- 14:23
- 14:24

Parents

- 1:8-9
- 4:1-4
- 10:1
- 13:1
- 13:24
- 15:5
- 15:20

Pastors

- 15:2

Prayer

- 3:5-6
- 15:8
- 15:29

Politics

- 11:14
- 12:3
- 14:28
- 14:34
- 14:35

Popularity

- 12:9

Service

- 3:27-28
- 11:17

Sex

- 5:1-23
- 6:25
- 6:26
- 6:27-29
- 6:30-35
- 7:1-27

Sin

- 1:10-18
- 10:23
- 10:24
- 15:15
- 15:21

Speech

- 4:24
- 10:11
- 10:13
- 10:18
- 10:19
- 10:20
- 10:21
- 10:31-32
- 11:9
- 11:12
- 12:6
- 12:13
- 12:16
- 12:18
- 13:2
- 13:3
- 14:3
- 15:1
- 15:4

Success

- 1:1-6
- 2:7-8
- 3:13
- 4:25-27
- 6:6-8
- 6:9-11
- 10:3
- 10:5

- 10:28
- 10:30
- 11:6
- 11:23
- 11:27
- 13:12
- 13:19
- 14:8
- 14:14
- 14:18
- 15:16

Text messaging

- 13:17

Trust

- 11:13
- 12:5

Wisdom

- 1:20-33
- 2:12
- 2:13-15
- 3:19-20
- 3:21
- 3:22-26
- 4:5-6
- 4:7-9
- 4:11
- 4:12
- 4:13
- 8:1-36
- 9:1
- 9:2-6
- 9:11
- 9:12
- 9:13-18

Endnotes

Chapter One

1. Proverbs, *The Preacher's Outline and Sermon Bible* (Alpha-Omega Ministries, Inc: 2012), 32.

2. Jim Newheiser, *Opening up Proverbs* (Day One Publications 2008), 20.

3. Charles R. Swindol, *Living the Proverbs Insight for the Daily Grind* (Worthy Publishing 2012), 7.

Chapter Two

1. Proverbs, *The Preacher's Outline and Sermon Bible* (Alpha-Omega Ministries, Inc: 2012), 61.

2. Jim Newheiser, *Opening up Proverbs* (Day One Publications 2008), 45.

3. Charles R. Swindol, *Living the Proverbs Insight for the Daily Grind* (Worthy Publishing 2012), 32.

Chapter Three

1. Proverbs, *The Preacher's Outline and Sermon Bible* (Alpha-Omega Ministries, Inc: 2012), 79.

2. Jim Newheiser, *Opening up Proverbs* (Day One Publications 2008), 59.

3. Charles R. Swindol, *Living the Proverbs Insight for the Daily Grind* (Worthy Publishing 2012), 40.

Chapter Four

1. Proverbs, *The Preacher's Outline and Sermon Bible* (Alpha-Omega Ministries, Inc: 2012), 93.

2. Jim Newheiser, *Opening up Proverbs* (Day One Publications 2008), 76

3. Charles R. Swindol, *Living the Proverbs Insight for the Daily Grind* (Worthy Publishing 2012), 50.

Chapter Five

1. Proverbs, *The Preacher's Outline and Sermon Bible* (Alpha-Omega Ministries, Inc: 2012), 103.

2. Jim Newheiser, *Opening up Proverbs* (Day One Publications 2008), 72.

Chapter Six

1. Proverbs, *The Preacher's Outline and Sermon Bible* (Alpha-Omega Ministries, Inc: 2012), 114.

2. Jim Newheiser, *Opening up Proverbs* (Day One Publications 2008), 72.

3. Charles R. Swindol, *Living the Proverbs Insight for the Daily Grind* (Worthy Publishing 2012), 117.

Chapter Seven

1. Proverbs, *The Preacher's Outline and Sermon Bible* (Alpha-Omega Ministries, Inc: 2012), 124.

2. Jim Newheiser, *Opening up Proverbs* (Day One Publications 2008), 73.

3. Charles R. Swindol, *Living the Proverbs Insight for the Daily Grind* (Worthy Publishing 2012), 118.

Chapter Eight

1. Proverbs, *The Preacher's Outline and Sermon Bible* (Alpha-Omega Ministries, Inc: 2012), 135.

2. Jim Newheiser, *Opening up Proverbs* (Day One Publications 2008), 87.

Chapter Nine

1. Proverbs, *The Preacher's Outline and Sermon Bible* (Alpha-Omega Ministries, Inc: 2012), 148.

2. Jim Newheiser, *Opening up Proverbs* (Day One Publications 2008), 50

Chapter Ten

1. Proverbs, *The Preacher's Outline and Sermon Bible* (Alpha-Omega Ministries, Inc: 2012), 170.

2. Jim Newheiser, *Opening up Proverbs* (Day One Publications 2008), 111.

Chapter Eleven

1. Raymond C. Ortlund Jr., *Proverbs Wisdom that Works* (Crossway 2012), 46.

2. John A. Kitchen, *Proverbs a Mentor Commentary* (Christian Focus Publications Ltd 2006), 241.

Chapter Twelve

1. Raymond C. Ortlund Jr., *Proverbs Wisdom that Works* (Crossway 2012), 182.

2. John A. Kitchen, *Proverbs a Mentor Commentary* (Christian Focus Publications Ltd 2006), 264.

Chapter Thirteen

1. Raymond C. Ortlund Jr., *Proverbs Wisdom that Works* (Crossway 2012), 176.

2. John A. Kitchen, *Proverbs a Mentor Commentary* (Christian Focus Publications Ltd 2006), 295.

Chapter Fourteen

1. Raymond C. Ortlund Jr., *Proverbs Wisdom that Works* (Crossway 2012), 23.

2. John A. Kitchen, *Proverbs a Mentor Commentary* (Christian Focus Publications Ltd 2006), 302.

Chapter Fifteen

1. Raymond C. Ortlund Jr., *Proverbs Wisdom that Works* (Crossway 2012), 177.

2. John A. Kitchen, *Proverbs a Mentor Commentary* (Christian Focus Publications Ltd 2006), 326.

Chapter Sixteen

1. Raymond C. Ortlund Jr., *Proverbs Wisdom that Works* (Crossway 2012), 182.

2. John A. Kitchen, *Proverbs a Mentor Commentary* (Christian Focus Publications Ltd 2006), 367.

Chapter Seventeen

1. Raymond C. Ortlund Jr., *Proverbs Wisdom that Works* (Crossway 2012), 166.

2. John A. Kitchen, *Proverbs a Mentor Commentary* (Christian Focus Publications Ltd 2006), 376.

Chapter Eighteen

1. Raymond C. Ortlund Jr., *Proverbs Wisdom that Works* (Crossway 2012), 134.

2. John A. Kitchen, *Proverbs a Mentor Commentary* (Christian Focus Publications Ltd 2006), 393.

Chapter Nineteen

1. Raymond C. Ortlund Jr., *Proverbs Wisdom that Works* (Crossway 2012), 182.

2. John A. Kitchen, *Proverbs a Mentor Commentary* (Christian Focus Publications Ltd 2006), 422.

Chapter Twenty

1. Raymond C. Ortlund Jr., *Proverbs Wisdom that Works* (Crossway 2012), 166.

2. John A. Kitchen, *Proverbs a Mentor Commentary* (Christian Focus Publications Ltd 2006), 443.

Chapter Twenty-One

1. Proverbs, *The Preacher's Outline and Sermon Bible* (Alpha-Omega Ministries, Inc: 2012), 329.

2. Raymond C. Ortlund Jr., *Proverbs Wisdom that Works* (Crossway 2012), 170.

3. John A. Kitchen, *Proverbs a Mentor Commentary* (Christian Focus Publications Ltd 2006), 468.

Chapter Twenty-Two, Twenty-Three, Twenty- Four.

1. Proverbs, *The Preacher's Outline and Sermon Bible* (Alpha-Omega Ministries, Inc: 2012), 356.

2. Raymond C. Ortlund Jr., *Proverbs Wisdom that Works* (Crossway 2012), 153.

3. John A. Kitchen, *Proverbs a Mentor Commentary* (Christian Focus Publications Ltd 2006), 500.

Chapter Twenty-five

1. Proverbs, *The Preacher's Outline and Sermon Bible* (Alpha-Omega Ministries, Inc: 2012), 388.

2. Raymond C. Ortlund Jr., *Proverbs Wisdom that Works* (Crossway 2012), 20.

3. John A. Kitchen, *Proverbs a Mentor Commentary* (Christian Focus Publications Ltd 2006), 571.

Chapter Twenty-Six

1. Proverbs, *The Preacher's Outline and Sermon Bible* (Alpha-Omega Ministries, Inc: 2012), 397.

2. Raymond C. Ortlund Jr., *Proverbs Wisdom that Works* (Crossway 2012), 100.

3. John A. Kitchen, *Proverbs a Mentor Commentary* (Christian Focus Publications Ltd 2006), 588.

Chapter Twenty-Seven

1. Proverbs, *The Preacher's Outline and Sermon Bible* (Alpha-Omega Ministries, Inc: 2012), 410.

2. Raymond C. Ortlund Jr., *Proverbs Wisdom that Works* (Crossway 2012), 22.

3. John A. Kitchen, *Proverbs a Mentor Commentary* (Christian Focus Publications Ltd 2006), 608.

Chapter Twenty-Eight

1. Proverbs, *The Preacher's Outline and Sermon Bible* (Alpha-Omega Ministries, Inc: 2012), 419.

2. Raymond C. Ortlund Jr., *Proverbs Wisdom that Works* (Crossway 2012), 178.

3. John A. Kitchen, *Proverbs a Mentor Commentary* (Christian Focus Publications Ltd 2006), 629.

Chapter Twenty-Nine

1. Proverbs, *The Preacher's Outline and Sermon Bible* (Alpha-Omega Ministries, Inc: 2012), 437.

2. Raymond C. Ortlund Jr., *Proverbs Wisdom that Works* (Crossway 2012), 132.

3. John A. Kitchen, *Proverbs a Mentor Commentary* (Christian Focus Publications Ltd 2006), 653.

Chapter Thirty

1. Raymond C. Ortlund Jr., *Proverbs Wisdom that Works* (Crossway 2012), 179.

2. John A. Kitchen, *Proverbs a Mentor Commentary* (Christian Focus Publications Ltd 2006), 678.

Chapter Thirty-One

1. Raymond C. Ortlund Jr., *Proverbs Wisdom that Works* (Crossway 2012), 179.

2. John A. Kitchen, *Proverbs a Mentor Commentary* (Christian Focus Publications Ltd 2006), 150.